Total Recall

D1388785

Total Recall

PERFECT RESPONSE TRAINING
FOR PUPPIES AND ADULT DOGS

PIPPA MATTINSON

Quiller

First published in the UK in 2012
by Quiller, an imprint of Quiller Publishing Ltd
Reprinted 2013 (twice), 2014, 2015 (twice), 2016 (twice), 2017, 2018 (twice), 2019 (twice)

British Library Cataloguing-in-Publication Data
A catalogue record for this book is available from the British Library

ISBN 978 1 84689 149 6

Design and typesetting by Paul Saunders
Printed in China

Quiller

An imprint of Quiller Publishing Ltd
Wykey House, Wykey, Shrewsbury, SY4 1JA
Tel: 01939 261616
Email: info@quillerbooks.com
Website: www.quillerpublishing.com

Contents

Acknowledgements   7

Introduction   8

Part 1 Preparation   11

1 A New Beginning   12

2 How Dogs Learn   18

3 Punishment and Reward   30

4 Practical Training with Rewards   40

5 All About Proofing   48

6 Beyond Training   55

7 Your Dog   64

8 Are You Ready?   69

Part 2 Training the Recall   81

9 Puppy Recall   82

10 Pre-recall for Older Dogs   94

11 Basic Recall   104

12 Proofing with People   116

13 Proofing with Dogs   128

14 On Location   141

15 Putting it All Together   156

16 Recall for Life   166

Part 3 Problem Solving   171

17 Where Did I Go Wrong?   172

18 Out of Control?   181

19 The Absconder   191

20 The About Turn Walk   201

21 The Artful Dodger   209

22 Using a Training Lead   214

23 Getting Active with Your Dog   224

24 The Finish   233

Useful Resources   241

Index   244

Acknowledgements

I am indebted to my sister, Sandra, and two daughters, Sam and Lucy, for their long hours spent proofreading and for their thoughtful comments. And to my husband, Duncan, and sons, Toby and Tom, for taking care of our home, and my dogs, whilst I immersed myself in this project.

I would also like to thank Jeff Boston, Carole Creech, and my entire family for their enthusiastic support and encouragement.

Photograph credits
The photos on pages 22, 35, 46, 72, 99, 101, 112, 133, 183, 199, 204, 217, 230 are by the author; those on pages 60, 118, 131, 138, 146, 152, 169, 194, 227 are by Nick Ridley; those on pages 84 and 92 are by Jeff Boston.

Introduction

Teaching your dog an effective recall is crucial if life with the dog is to be a pleasure. In the UK at least, letting a dog off the lead is the norm, and getting him back on it again without tears is essential for his owner's sanity.

This is a book for all dog owners. It is written for those who battle with the daily misery of a dog that won't come back when he is called, and it is written for those with new puppies who want to get a good recall established from the very start.

When I first started out in gundog training over thirty years ago, the standard procedure when a dog ignored the recall command was to 'get out' after the dog and to catch and punish him at the scene of the crime. There are a number of drawbacks to this kind of approach, and some trainers began to look for more pleasant and effective alternatives.

Times have now changed and most dog trainers have moved on. People no longer want to shake and smack their dogs. The sight of a large person physically and publicly chastising a small dog (should they be lucky enough to catch him) is no longer considered acceptable. You don't want to be that person, and you don't need to be, in order to get your dog to come back to you when you call him.

There is another way, and that is what this book is all about.

Total Recall focuses firmly on the most important skill you will ever teach your dog. It explains how to use modern reward-based dog training methods effectively, and does so in plain English. It walks you step-by-step through the process of creating a powerful and permanent recall, in all manner of different and distracting situations.

This book is divided into three parts. In Part One you will find all the information you need to prepare and support you as you work through the programme. At its core, in Part Two, you will find a detailed Recall Training Programme complete with exercises for you to work through – the 'how to' section of the book. In Part Three you will find a *Problem Solving* section. This is where you can discover how you got into difficulties in the past, and learn how to avoid making the same mistakes again.

You will need to read the *Preparation* chapters in order to use the training programme, but you can skip the *Problem Solving* section if your dog is a model student. You will also find plenty of resources listed in the back of the book to help you. Enjoy your training journey and above all, have fun with your dog!

Pippa Mattinson

PART **1**

Preparation

- A New Beginning

- How Dogs Learn

- Punishment and Reward

- Practical Training with Rewards

- All About Proofing

- Beyond Training

- Your Dog

- Are You Ready?

CHAPTER 1

A New Beginning

N o other animal shares human lives in quite such an intimate way as dogs. No other large and powerful species of animal is allowed such unrestricted access to our homes and families, and to the wider community, or is permitted such close contact with children and other vulnerable members of our society. Welcoming a dog into your home for the first time is a life-changing moment. Owning a dog has the potential to enhance your life in so many ways. Yet, because of the intimate way that dogs move among us, there is also great potential for your dog to seriously disrupt your world.

Dogs need to form good relationships with their owners if they are to become pleasant and enjoyable members of our society. A dog does not know how to choose behaviour that is appropriate in the human community; it is essential that his human partner is able to make those choices for him. Unless your dog is to spend his life restrained or indoors, the power to make those choices depends absolutely on your ability to recall your dog at any time. Unfortunately, for many dog owners, recall training is an art that proves far more difficult to master than they had anticipated.

Great expectations

Preparing to bring your dog home for the first time is an exciting experience. Each prospective dog owner has his or her own hopes, dreams and expectations for the new life ahead. The sight of your dog bounding happily towards you across the fields, relaxing evenings by the fire as he sleeps at your feet, daily walks through the forest with him trotting along at your side, these are all the kind of natural expectations you may have of life as a dog owner. It is probably safe to assume that shouting yourself hoarse, weeping with frustration over the empty lead in your hand, or silently cursing as you watch the tail end of your dog slide gracefully over the horizon for the tenth time in a week, did not feature prominently in your daydreams. Yet, for many owners of a young dog, these typical frustrations of an inadequate or absent recall are a grim reality – the daily walks so eagerly anticipated are in fact about as enjoyable as a visit to the dentist.

You may be reading this book because you already have a recall problem with your dog, or perhaps because you want to avoid one by getting your recall training properly established right from the beginning. As with most aspects of life, prevention of recall problems is always better than cure. But let's face it, often we don't realise we have a problem until it is too late to take avoidance action. That is why this book deals not only with creating a superb recall the easy way (starting with a new puppy), but also with helping those of you who have gone astray somewhere along the recall training path.

We all have such good intentions about training our dogs when they are small. Some of you will have booked classes and bought books even before you brought your new puppy home. Yet all too often our good intentions fall by the wayside.

One of the reasons that many people abandon their dog training, whether they are attending classes or learning from books, is a lack of confidence and trust in the system they are using, and in the methods that they are being advised to apply. Nowadays we tend to regard our dogs as 'friends' and 'members of the family'. We want to enjoy training them and to treat them kindly. Yet some trainers, and some training systems, have failed to recognise this important development, and many new puppy owners are put off training their pets after observing harsh methods or aggressive handling.

Others abandon their training efforts because training seems complicated and dull, or because the results are far from satisfactory and fail to translate to the real world of walks in public places, unexpected visitors, day trips and school runs.

Training a dog successfully in the modern world requires a system that is at once compassionate, effective and fun. A dog training system must provide these three elements in order to be a success with modern dog owners – at the heart of any great partnership between a human being and a dog lies an effective and reliable recall.

You are not alone

If you are already getting into difficulties with your dog, don't be too hard on yourself. When your dog is embarrassing you by ignoring your whistles, when he is cavorting about annoying other people, it can seem as though every other dog in the world is better behaved than yours. This is simply not the case. The fact is, despite a wealth of 'how to' books and the availability of dog training classes in almost every village hall up and down the country, a lot of people are still struggling with their dogs. The letters and emails I receive show me that, in most cases, what people want more than anything else is for their dog to come back when he is called. Yet this seemingly simple act is a major stumbling block for a significant proportion of dog owners.

Why is it so hard to teach a good recall?

In the old days, training methods were fairly straightforward. The dog got a pat on the head when he was good and a clip round the ear when he was bad. Sometimes the dog got trained, sometimes the dog just got hardened to being clipped around the ear, or very good at dodging.

For modern dog owners, life is a little more complicated. People nowadays think a lot more about what they are doing, and about how their dog is feeling. Most people want to train their dogs with a minimum amount of punishment. This is a good thing, especially with recall where, by definition, the dog is usually out of reach of the handler and therefore difficult to correct in a timely way. Reward-based training now leads the way in most dog sports and dog training disciplines. However, if we want to successfully train with as few corrections as possible, it is vital that we control the consequences of the dog's behaviour very closely and use rewards effectively, which many people fail to do.

As every new dog owner rapidly discovers, you and your dog have a very different agenda. The two of you are never going to agree on what is important. Being on time for a business meeting or collecting the children from school do not rate highly on your dog's list of priorities. You are never going to appreciate the finer points of eating horse manure, nor will he ever appreciate your obsession for walking at a snail's pace, or for going home just as he is beginning to enjoy himself. But if you can understand and accept what truly matters to your dog, what is valuable to him, half the battle is won before you even begin training.

The truth is that it isn't actually difficult to teach a reliable recall in a modern and positive way if you are armed with the right information and have access to a structured training system.

A structured system

Humans have a remarkable ability to generalise their learning. This means that they can take a skill that they have learned in one place, and apply that knowledge and learning in a completely different place, or in a completely different context. We tend to assume (wrongly) that dogs can do this too.

Dogs, on the other hand, initially have great difficulty in taking skills that they have learned in a given situation, and applying those same skills to a different situation. This gets them into no end of trouble. Often a dog owner thinks he has taught his dog a great recall, only to be dismayed when the dog abandons him in favour of other dogs or people, in the park or on the beach. Dogs simply cannot comprehend that the recall command they learned in the garden also applies in the countryside, or when there are other dogs to play with. The solution to this difficulty is carefully structured training, so that the recall is built up in 'layers', each layer a little more challenging than the last.

This is why I have provided, in Part Two, a clearly laid out system to lead you through the recall training process in a very detailed and structured way. You will learn how to build an effective recall command from the foundations up. Layer by layer, and step by step.

The remaining chapters in this first part of the book are designed to ensure that you have all the information and knowledge that you need to work through the training programme effectively. This 'preparation' is important and separating it from the training instructions will help to ensure that the training programme itself is not muddled up with too many explanations and too much background information.

Understanding how dogs think

Teaching your dog to come back when you call him is about changing the way he behaves in response to your signal or command. When you first call or whistle your dog, he has no idea that the signal you have just given has any meaning whatsoever, and his behaviour reflects that. When we train a dog to respond to a command in a specific way (coming towards us when we whistle, for example), we are changing or modifying his future behaviour. Fortunately for us, a huge amount of research has been carried out in behaviour modification, and the results of this research are freely available and very useful to dog owners.

In order for you to change your dog's future behaviour you first need to understand what motivates him to behave as he does. Few people have the time and inclination to become an expert in animal psychology in order to train their dogs, and so in the next chapter, *How Dogs Learn*, I have put together the information that will help you get inside your dog's head and understand what influences the decisions he makes.

Is it worth the effort?

While embarking on a training programme may seem a little daunting, you will never regret the time you invest in teaching your dog to come when you call him. A good recall has the potential to remove your dog from harm's way, and even save his life. It will certainly prevent him from being a nuisance to others and will keep him out of mischief on a regular basis. It will, in fact, be used and appreciated every single day that you spend with your dog.

The difficulties that many new dog owners experience with recall training not only affect the owners, but the dogs too – many out-of-control dogs end up in rescue centres. Abandonment of dogs is a huge problem in the UK and many, if not most, abandoned dogs have training issues.

Teaching your dog an effective recall, and recommending this book to others so that they can do the same, will help to promote the pleasures and benefits of responsible dog ownership. The warm glow of pride you experience each time your dog obeys you in public will never go away, and your new skill will also open up other opportunities for you to interact with, and enjoy, your dog.

CHAPTER 2

How Dogs Learn

Over the last two hundred years or so, our relationship with dogs has become increasingly complex. Dogs have become involved as assistants in many aspects of human life: herding sheep; acting as eyes and ears for humans in need; helping to provide food as hunting companions; sniffing out drugs and explosives; apprehending criminals and much more.

So how is it that some people seem to be able to train dogs to carry out incredibly complex tasks, while others are engaged in an unsuccessful and daily battle of wills just to stop their dog from jumping up at visitors? Is there some kind of natural talent with dogs that only a few of us are endowed with? Are some people just destined to be great dog trainers while others are doomed to be dragged around on the end of a lead like a ball and chain?

During the last century, the academic study of animal behaviour, conducted by scientists, has produced a wealth of information about how animals learn new and different ways to behave. The information shows unequivocally that the skills which will enable you to train your dog are not a mystical talent, but can indeed be learnt by anyone. Although the results of many of these studies have been available for a long time, it has only been recently that much of this knowledge has been embraced, and applied, by dog trainers – there are still many trainers that reject or ignore the information we now have at our disposal.

A touch of magic

I believe that the resistance to making use of behavioural science is partly because we all have a natural inclination to buy into romantic notions of gifted animal trainers with special skills – people who are able to 'speak the language' of dogs and horses. We like to believe that there is a little touch of magic in animal training, that the brilliant trainer has some kind of natural ability that others lack. Dog trainers sometimes give themselves names that imply such a special gift. Names like Whisperer or Listener lend a mysterious air to the whole business of dog training and there is, perhaps, a reluctance for successful trainers to have that 'magic' stripped away. Many people see dog training as an art rather than a science, and would prefer it to remain that way.

It is my personal belief that this approach does a disservice to dog owners and deprives people of the information and understanding that they need to have healthy and successful relationships with their dogs. I want to make it clear to you right now that you do not need to possess any kind of 'talent' in order to achieve an excellent recall with your dog.

The only difference between those who are successful in dog train-ing and those who are not is the consistent application of well-timed and appropriate consequences to their dog's actions. Whether the dog owner learns to do this by reading this book, by copying another trainer, by studying animal psychology, or just happens across the technique by chance is not very relevant. The important thing to remember is that if they can do it, so can you. Of course, some people will pick this skill up more quickly than others – just as one person takes to the practical side of driving a car more easily than another, some take to dog training more easily. It may take you a little longer, but once you have achieved a great recall, no one will know the difference between you and your local 'whisperer'.

Why the science matters

While the 'art' of a dog trainer lies in the way he has learnt to apply his methods with skill and precision, the techniques he uses are based on solid science. Understanding some of the concepts of the science of behaviour is crucial in enabling those who may not have the professional trainer's experience or natural abilities to successfully train their dog. Understanding these concepts need not be boring or difficult, as we shall see.

Everything that people or animals do can be broken down into tiny steps or component parts. This is one of the key elements of all successful modern training programmes in any discipline. Another key is understanding what motivates behaviour and learning to manipulate it. It is this key that behavioural science has handed us on a plate, and we ignore it at great cost.

If your dog has not been coming back when you call him, we need to change this. And understanding what makes a dog change his behaviour is vital. For that reason, the first task of this chapter is to discover exactly what makes a dog decide to alter his behaviour, to act in a new and different way rather than carrying out the same old actions he has carried out in the past. Once we can understand what drives changes in our dog's behaviour, we can begin to control the way he behaves in the future.

But before we look at what is driving your dog's decisions, and how we can modify his behaviour, we first need to have a look at his limitations.

Your dog's limitations

If you are to achieve Total Recall with your dog, you need to take a long hard look at just what is going on inside his head, because it is possibly a great deal less than you imagine.

Relatively speaking, dogs are uncomplicated creatures not overly endowed with intellectual or problem-solving skills. Before you leap to their defence, I should point out that a lot of suffering has been inflicted on dogs as a result of human insistence on believing in the 'super abilities' of their innocent companions.

As humans have become ever more enamoured and involved with their four-footed friends, they have in some cases credited dogs with abilities and characteristics which they simply do not possess, and this has not always been to a dog's advantage. Guilt, remorse, even malicious intent and criminal tendencies have all been attributed to dogs! Studies show that it is unlikely that dogs experience emotions in the same way as humans, yet many dog owners remain unconvinced.

What we do know is that dogs learn like other mammals, including ourselves, through experiencing the consequences of their actions and modifying their future actions accordingly.

We will look at this in more detail in a moment. Generally speaking, all animals 'repeat in the future' behaviours that have led to a rewarding consequence in the past, and 'avoid in the future' behaviours that have led to unpleasant consequences in the past. This essential behavioural characteristic helps to ensure the survival of each species in an ever-changing environment.

However, unlike people, dogs are not able to rationalise what they have learnt. They don't ponder on what you have taught them and apply this knowledge to new experiences. For this simple reason a dog that has learned to 'sit' in his own kitchen will often disappoint when asked to show off his new skill in a neighbour's kitchen. He is not being naughty, he has just not grasped that the command word 'sit' means the same thing in your neighbour's kitchen as it does in his own.

Dogs do not have a 'moral compass' to give them boundaries for acceptable behaviour. A dog cannot ever be a 'thief' even though we call him one when he steals our breakfast from the kitchen table. He cannot be a thief because he has no concept of possession. He only understands consequences. Stealing breakfast in front of 'The Boss' may get him a telling off, but stealing breakfast while she is answering the phone gets him bacon and eggs! Two very different consequences. The first one teaches the dog not to steal in front of 'The Boss'. The second one teaches him that stealing when 'The Boss' is out of the room is OK. In all likelihood, he probably learns something else. He probably learns that sometimes 'The Boss' comes into the room after she has been on the phone, and behaves in a most unreasonable fashion, shouting at him and stabbing her finger at an empty plate, even sending him unceremoniously outside to stand in the rain (just as well he has something warm in his tummy).

When 'The Boss' becomes angry and unreasonable, the dog will normally make himself look small and subservient. This is what dogs do automatically when a powerful dog (or person) becomes aggressive. 'The Boss', on the other hand, seeing the dog fling himself on the floor with his paws over his ears, reads this behaviour as 'guilt'. The dog, by the way, has no idea that this rant is about the bacon and eggs he ate, because that happened five minutes ago. This brings us to the question of timing.

Dogs do not have a moral code

The importance of timing

One of the things our twentieth-century behaviourists discovered was that the consequences of a behaviour only affected the likelihood of that behaviour being repeated in the future if the consequences follow the behaviour immediately. I am talking seconds here, not minutes. This is actually important for the survival of the animal. In nature, a consequence is normally only connected to an action if it takes place in the same time frame. If you fall in a pond, you get wet there and then, you don't get wet five minutes after you climb out! So if you don't like getting wet, you learn to stay away from ponds. Humans have introduced the concept of delayed consequences, waiting outside the headmaster's study for a punishment, or waiting until the end of the month for a salary. It works for us to a certain extent because we can mull things over in our heads and hold onto a thought or concept in our minds. This, however, requires the complexities of language, and trying to apply delayed consequences to a dog is like banging your head on a brick wall. It won't stop hurting until you stop doing it.

Dogs learn best when the people around them 'dish out' consequences in a logical, immediate and predictable way. This also works best for people, but that is another story! Before we look more closely at how we can use consequences to modify our dogs' behaviour, it is worth mentioning the question of dominance and leadership.

Pack theory and dominance

A lot of people get very wound up about theories of dominance, or needing to be a pack leader. These are concepts upon which a number of traditional dog training styles are based, and which arouse very strong feelings among many modern dog trainers who see them as outdated and unproven.

Some dog training systems are still heavily focused on dominating dogs – you will hear all sorts of advice about how to become dominant over your dog. Some dog trainers believe that dogs view their family as a 'wolf pack' with the hierarchy implicit in pack social structure. Others believe that pack theory does not apply to domestic dogs at all. Fortunately it doesn't actually matter who is right, because training dogs is all about behaviour modification, and behaviour modification is about controlling the consequences of behaviour, not about delving into its origins.

You don't need to worry about being a pack leader in order to train your dog. Be assured that most modern domestic dogs have no interest in taking over your family, they simply like to do what they enjoy, which is mostly eating, running around and rolling in things, and will find the quickest, easiest way in which to engage in those activities.

Just focus on the training. If you are keen on leadership, remember that a leader is simply the individual in control of resources. Unless your dog has opposable thumbs and a credit card, that would be you. You will find that leadership falls nicely into place once you take responsibility for all of the resources available to your dog, by controlling the consequences of your dog's behaviour.

Drives and instincts

Some of your dog's behaviour is instinctive rather than learned. The sort of instincts that come bundled with your dog will depend partly on his breeding. Dogs bred for coursing (greyhounds and whippets, for example) and some working bred gundogs, have quite a strong instinctive chase response to moving objects. You will probably have read about 'this drive' and 'that drive' all of which is very interesting, especially if you are breeding dogs to develop particular instincts or characteristics. However, delving into the history or breed specific characteristics of your dog won't influence the order and structure of your recall training programme at all. Your dog's temperament or urges may affect the time it takes you to get your dog through some of the stages in training because these instincts may function as an extra distraction for him, but he will still have to go through those same stages in training, no matter what his temperament. Where drives and instincts may come in handy is in helping you choose rewards for your dog. We will look at rewards in greater detail in chapter four.

Using consequences to change our dog's behaviour

So, we have established that the primary motivating force for animal behaviour is the consequences that the animal is expecting after carrying out that behaviour. This simple truth is the core of the scientific explanation for how all higher animals learn, and the key to modifying animal behaviour, or in our case to training dogs to come when they are called.

To get to grips with how this 'game' of consequences works in practice, we need to look a bit more closely at the science.

Basically, an action carried out by an animal can have three possible consequences:

- Things can get better for the dog

- Things can get worse for the dog

- Things can stay the same

Let's suppose your dog wants to go out into the garden. If your dog scratches at the door and you open it, things just got better for him. If your dog scratches at the door and you say 'No! Bad dog' things just got worse. If your dog scratches at the door and you ignore him, things stayed the same. In the last two cases he will be less likely to scratch the door in the future; in the first example, he is more likely to scratch the door next time.

But of course we don't want to just increase the probability or likelihood of the right response, we are looking for certainty and reliability. We want a recall that works every single time. Fortunately, repeated applications of consequences result in a dog developing a 'trained response' or habit of always responding appropriately to our signals.

Taking control of consequences

These simple rules of behaviour apply universally, whether you are in your kitchen, in a laboratory or in the middle of a twenty-acre field. However, to train a dog effectively you must have full control over the consequences of your dog's behaviour, and this is a good deal easier in a confined space. Many people try to walk before they can run, by attempting to establish a new skill in a place where they have little or no control over the outcome of their dog's behaviour. This book shows you how to begin with the easiest exercises in situations where you have a lot of control, and moves you on gradually to more challenging environments as your control and influence over your dog increases.

Extinction

This section has nothing to do with dinosaurs; we are going to use the word extinction in the behavioural sense. Let's first take a look at the last of the three consequences mentioned previously, 'things stay the same'. Experiments have shown that if things stay the same (i.e. there are no consequences to the dog's actions) then that particular behaviour will die out. This phenomenon is called extinction. If a dog is displaying a behaviour that we do not like (such as ignoring us when we call him) then we are very happy for that behaviour to become extinct. On the other hand, if he is displaying a behaviour that we welcome, racing back to us at the toot of a whistle, then the last thing we want is for that behaviour to become extinct. For these reasons it is important for us to understand the potential for extinction and how we can encourage or prevent it.

It is relatively straightforward to demonstrate extinction in the controlled environment of a laboratory, but more challenging to do so in the real world where it is not always a simple matter to ensure that no consequence occurs. In the previous example, where we ignore the dog that is scratching at the door, it is quite likely that, in a family situation, someone else would come along and open the door for him, or give him a cuddle, or he might even spot half a sandwich under the table and help himself to that, thus putting paid to any hope of extinction taking place because these are all rewards for the dog, however accidental they may be.

Often when we think there will be no consequence there actually is one. There are so many simple things a dog can do to reward himself, from rolling on his back to chasing a cat. I'm sure you can think of others. The point is that, as we have seen, if the dog rewards himself immediately after some undesired behaviour that you were intending to ignore, extinction will not occur and your training will be adversely affected. Preventing this from happening can be problematical with recall training due to the distance between the dog and his trainer. We will look in more detail later at the challenges of controlling extinction, and how we can overcome them.

Incidentally, scientists refer to this 'game of consequences' as 'operant conditioning'. Every dog training system ever devised uses techniques to control one or more of the three consequences that we have discussed.

Reinforcers and punishers

Let's look at two key consequences again – a dog carries out an action and things get better or the dog carries out an action and things get worse. A reinforcer is something that makes things get better for the dog. A punisher is something that makes things get worse. When you open the door for a dog that was scratching it, the opening is the reinforcer. Another example of a reinforcer is food – if a dog sits on command and gets a biscuit, the biscuit is a reinforcer. When you give the dog a biscuit you are providing reinforcement for whatever he happened to be doing just before he got the reward, whether that was sitting quietly or something you might consider less desirable, like putting his feet on the table. Other common reinforcers are opportunities for activities that the dog enjoys, such as chasing and running. If you whistle your dog and then allow him to run around in circles for two minutes you have reinforced his behaviour, which was of course the act of ignoring your recall. He will therefore be even more likely to ignore your whistle next time.

An example of a punisher is pain. Many people think that they don't use punishment when they actually use it a lot – punishers don't have to be painful. A verbal rebuke such as 'Bad Dog!' can be a punisher for some dogs. Loud noises can be punishers if the dog doesn't like them, as can a squirt of water or a puff of air. It all depends on what the dog likes and doesn't like. For some dogs a verbal rebuke is a walk in the park, others will fall apart if you so much as raise an eyebrow at them. This is why it is important that you are clear on this because, crucially, what is a reinforcer (or a punisher) for one dog will not necessarily work for another. We look at the controversial topic of when and whether you should use punishment at all in the next chapter.

Controlling extinction, or ensuring that no consequences occur, often involves enclosing or restraining the dog in some way, to prevent him from reinforcing himself by indulging in a rewarding activity without your consent.

Rewards

Most people like the idea of reward-based training. Many reinforcers are what we ordinary folk call rewards. However, it is probably worth mentioning that scientists don't like the term 'rewards' and if you decide to read up on operant conditioning you will need to get used to the word reinforcer. This distinction is necessary because not all reinforcers are actually rewards. Sometimes we can reinforce behaviour by taking something away – this is called 'negative reinforcement'.

The word negative is used in its mathematical sense of subtracting something. An example of 'negative reinforcement' in dog training would be the practice of 'force fetching' used by some gundog trainers in the USA. In force fetching, the dog's ear is pinched hard enough to hurt. When the dog obeys the command to take hold of a dummy with his mouth, the pinch is released and the pain stops. This is negative reinforcement. The desired behaviour has been reinforced, but by taking something away (in this case pain) rather than by adding something. Most trainers in the UK do not use negative reinforcement in dog training, and if I say that you are going to 'reinforce' your dog's behaviour, I will always be referring to positive reinforcement, which we all know as rewards.

Some people worry that training which relies heavily on rewards is not effective. They are concerned about spoiling their dogs, and for this reason it is important that we understand exactly how rewards affect the training process and that when we do use rewards, we use them effectively. Crucial to the success of your training is your choice of rewards and we will look at this in more detail in the next chapter.

From theory to practice

'Now this theory is all very well...' I hear you saying '...you keep going on about consequences. This is beginning to look as though I am going to have to control the consequences of everything my dog does, every single time he does it, for the rest of his life. What kind of method is that?'

Obviously, if a dog owner had to reward his dog every single time the dog gets something right, and punish him or ignore him every single time he gets something wrong, training would be a huge and never-ending bore. Fortunately, scientists have done some useful research into how the frequency of reinforcers can be diminished. For example, we now know that not only is it ok not to reward your dog every single time he comes, interestingly it is better if you do not do so. All this and more will be explained in the next chapter, where we look at controlling consequences in more detail.

Your dog exhibits a vast range of behaviours every day. Some are more desirable than others! You now have a good understanding of what makes a particular behaviour more likely to increase or diminish in the future. This is the crucial first step in achieving an excellent recall response.

Let's move on now and find out how we can manipulate the consequences of your dog's behaviour to create a strong and reliable recall.

CHAPTER 3

Punishment and Reward

Punishments and rewards are commonly used consequences for shaping and changing animal behaviour. Punishment is a powerful word. For many it conjures up images of beatings and other forms of cruelty that were commonly perpetrated on children and dogs in a bygone era.

Until forty or fifty years ago, most serious dog training was carried out using fairly harsh methods. Largely, reward-based techniques were considered soft and ineffective. Slapping, beating and even kicking dogs were common behaviour. In short, we were not very nice to our dogs. As dogs have become more highly regarded, public demand for kinder training methods has increased. Violence and cruelty towards dogs are no longer considered acceptable and, happily, reward-based dog training has become the norm in many parts of the world.

Technically speaking, a punisher is simply anything which has the power to diminish a behaviour and needn't involve what most of us would consider cruelty at all. However, because the word punishment has so many unpleasant connotations, I think it is important to define what type of punishment we are talking about. While few pet dog trainers use harsh punishments nowadays, many use 'corrections' in some form or another. We use the word correction for a specific type of punishment: namely one that is not violent or distressing to a dog and that does not involve the kind of harsh treatment that most people would find unacceptable. It is this type of punishment, a verbal rebuke for example, which we will consider below.

Corrections

In principle, I have no problem with dog trainers who use corrections in training, provided that the corrections are proportionate and effective. But in practical terms it is not a simple matter of incorporating effective corrections into a recall training programme. This is partly because of the difficulties of correcting a dog in a timely manner when he is more than twenty yards away from you, and partly because corrections can inhibit the very response that we are trying to create.

Correcting a dog for ignoring a recall is fraught with difficulty. Some experienced and nimble trainers are able to 'run down' a dog and punish him effectively. By effectively I mean at, or near, the place where he committed an offence, and very soon afterwards. But the reality is that unless you are an Olympic sprinter with the cornering ability of a hare, or have a very obliging dog, your chances of correcting your dog effectively in open country are slim.

More importantly, correcting a dog can have side effects that directly interfere with recall. The problem is that corrections may make your dog wary of approaching you. This wariness may be temporary, but your dog is unlikely to want to come near you while he perceives that you are in a 'bad mood'. The dog's conclusions about your state of mind are not unreasonable when he has just observed you racing across a field towards him waving your arms wildly, shouting obscenities through clenched teeth.

A temporary aversion to your presence may not be a problem at all if you are simply trying to teach a dog to sit still where you left him, but it can seriously hamper your efforts to create a good recall response, for recall by definition requires the dog to finish up at your side.

The possibility of reducing your dog's enthusiasm for your company is not the only risk involved in correcting a dog. Ending up in a game of tag, with you in hot pursuit of the miscreant, may only serve to amuse your dog enough for a repeat performance. Remember that unless you are exceptionally intimidating, most dogs like being chased.

Bear in mind also that some dogs are extremely tough. For a correction to be effective it has to upset the dog to some degree. It must act as a punisher to diminish the likelihood of a repeat behaviour. But whilst you might be able to upset a golden retriever with a cross word, a terrier is likely to remain indifferent. How are you going to correct a dog that finds a scolding and even a scruff shake amusing? You can see how corrections, even with the best of intentions, can escalate to severe punishment and even abuse.

The reality is that punishment of any description is rarely a useful or effective tool in the recall training process. Our objective is to make sure that the dog wants to be next to his owner so much that he will move heaven and earth to get there. And the way we achieve that is through the cunning use of rewards.

About rewards

All trainers reward their dogs for good behaviour. Even the most traditional trainers use rewards for dogs in training, most often verbal praise and stroking or patting. However, the type of reward we use can be a bone of contention.

Experiments have shown that some of the most effective rewards in training animals are those that fulfil the animal's primary needs, such as food. Some dog owners struggle with the concept of using food in training. They feel that it is somehow cheating. They believe that the dog should really be obeying them out of loyalty and love. Remember the problems we discussed earlier, with endowing dogs with human emotions? The difficulty with relying on praise or stroking for a reward is that it assumes that a demonstration of human affection is the most desirable thing you can offer the dog. An exchange of affection is so important to people that they may naturally assume it is just as important to their dog.

In some cases this is nearly right. For some dogs, human contact (stroking, cuddling etc.) has a very high value. Certain breeds and certain individuals are just far more interested in physical human contact and approval than others. The working bred cocker spaniels that I work with are often like this – they crave human affection and contact to an excessive degree. These dogs will work hard to obtain affection from humans, at least in the early stages of training. We tend to describe these types of dogs as 'biddable'. However, once training becomes more challenging and temptations abound, the trained responses of even biddable dogs may begin to crumble. This is often where punishment is first introduced. After all, the dog is trained and should know better... shouldn't he?

Many dogs are never particularly biddable. That is to say, they place little value on petting and stroking or human approval in general, unless there is absolutely nothing else whatever to do. So whilst your dog may like to sit with his head on your lap having his ears rumpled in the evenings while you watch TV, as soon as someone knocks at the door, or when he is out in the park, he has about as much interest in having his ears rumpled as you do. You can see how hard it will be to train an action-focused dog in these situations if you insist on using ear rumpling as one of your rewards – you have about as much chance of success as I do in trying to persuade someone to mend my car in exchange for pebbles. Attempting to train a dog that has little interest in praise or touch outdoors, without food or some other attractive reward, inevitably leads to either punishment (to prevent the bad behaviour) or failed training.

Using food as a reward

Food is a primary reward – one of life's fundamental necessities – and access to food is easily controlled by humans. This makes it a good training aid. Some 'old school' professional trainers abhor the use of food, largely because they are often unaware that using food rewards does not mean handing out biscuits every time the dog obeys a command. In fact, you can't take a dog and a bag of biscuits and then feed him every time you call him and expect him to keep coming back. In the long run he won't. Rewards do not work like that. We will find out just why that is, and how we can use food effectively in training without being tied to it forever. Many people now avoid punishing their dogs and want to focus on reward-based training. Yet they immediately handicap themselves by their refusal to consider food as a choice of reward, expecting instead that their dogs should behave appropriately in return for human affection. But as we have seen, not all dogs are capable of this. Clinging on to the view that food is cheating can be a big stumbling block for you if you let it.

Unsurprisingly, many older dogs will ignore food outdoors. This is quite normal if food has not been used much during their basic training. The rewards normally available to dogs outdoors (hunting, chasing and running) are more valuable to dogs than something pulled from your pocket. This problem can be overcome if the dog is properly retrained from the beginning, paying attention to the gambling effect described on page 36, and initially offered substantial and attractive rewards when outdoors. Because it fulfils a basic biological need, dogs quickly get used to working with food if this takes place on a regular basis and correct foundations are established for advanced training. Using food in this way is not cheating, it is just good sense.

Your choice of food will depend partly on what you feed your dog normally. Mine are fed on raw meat, so I can use dry kibble (pelleted dog food) as rewards. This is easy to carry about and is a real treat for them. However, if like most dogs, yours is fed on kibble for his normal meals, you will need to find something more interesting to use as a reward. Pick something your dog really loves. Tiny cubes of cheese or toast are popular examples and you can find recipes online for interesting 'liver cakes' which you bake in the oven and cut into little squares yourself. If you believe that your dog is not motivated by food then you need to rethink what you are offering the dog to eat. Dry toast or dog biscuits do not appeal to all dogs, some will require something more extravagant to catch their interest. Chunks of roast ham, pork or chicken, for example, are rarely ignored by even the most food-indifferent of dogs.

The food needs to be easily accessible so that there is no delay between the dog arriving in front of you and him getting his treat. A pocket in an

Little cubes of cheese and toast make good basic recall rewards

old coat is fine for dry food, but for tasty morsels you will need a dedicated little bag that you attach to your belt or clip around your waist. You can line this with a plastic food bag to save washing it. Once your dog is used to working for food outdoors, each basic reward should be really tiny, not much bigger than a pea. He will still find it rewarding, and this enables you to give a lot of rewards without filling him up or making him fat.

Will I be a walking larder?

Now you may be wondering if you will have to be a walking larder for the rest of your dog's life and the answer is no, you will not. Constant rewards are ineffective in the long term and carrying sacks of food everywhere you go would be highly inconvenient. Fortunately for us, nature has devised a better way.

Let's look at a useful feature of operant conditioning called the 'gambling effect', which enables us to reduce the frequency of rewards we offer the dog without diminishing the trained behaviour that we have so carefully established.

The gambling effect

The phenomenon known as the gambling effect was discovered many years ago. It is, however, a double-edged sword, providing both effective animal training and, sadly, human addiction. Let's look at how it works.

There are different ways to dish out rewards. You can give a reward every time an animal offers the behaviour you want. You say 'come', the dog comes, you give the dog a biscuit. The next time you say 'come' and he comes, you give him another biscuit.

Alternatively, you can take a slightly different approach and give the reward sometimes while withholding the reward at other times. We call this a variable schedule of reinforcement.

If you ask a dog to sit and reward him instantly, every time he does so, he will soon be sitting reliably. We call this a continuous schedule or reinforcement, and it is a good way to establish a new behaviour in the initial stages. But what happens if you keep rewarding him every time he sits, for months and months? Well, not only will you get through an awful lot of cheese or toast, surprisingly, in time, your dog's new behaviour may become unreliable. The continuous schedule of rewards is no longer effective in modifying or maintaining his behaviour. It has lost its power. How did that happen?

Addicted to recall

It is all linked to survival in the wild. If you take the same dog as we have just mentioned as the example, establish a reliable sit in exactly the same way, then begin rewarding him only some of the time, in an unpredictable way, hey presto, your training will remain reliable. The explanation for this behaviour lies in our environment, which is constantly changing. In the natural world animals may need to make several attempts at a task in order to get a reward, and they are most unlikely to be able to predict when that reward will arrive. A baby wildebeest may not be successful on his first attempt to cross a river after his mother has led the way. He may need to make three or four swims before he is rewarded by the safety of his reunion with her. This persistence in the face of intermittent rewards is absolutely essential for survival in the wild. An animal that gave up on anything that did not bring an instant reward would not survive for very long. As a result this powerful attraction to intermittent rewards has become literally programmed into most 'higher' animals, including us. Unfortunately, in humans, the gambling effect is responsible for a number of addictions – games and betting often supply the user with completely unpredictable and random rewards, thus triggering the gambling effect and causing addiction in the person engaging in the activity.

Happily for you, we want your dog to be addicted to recall, and can use the gambling effect to help us.

A word about bribes

One of the reasons that some dog trainers object to the use of food in dog training is because they see it as a bribe. No one wants to feel that their dog is only obeying them because he has been bribed to do so.

A bribe is something offered in advance of a specific behaviour, in order to increase the likelihood of that behaviour occurring. If you hold out a piece of food then ask a dog to sit, you are bribing him. This may be perfectly acceptable in the very early stages of training, especially if you want to manoeuvre the dog into a specific position, but is not a long-term solution to training. The problem with bribes is that the trainer is unable to control the dog when he does not have the bribe to offer. This is another good reason to use a variable schedule of reinforcement described earlier. A variable schedule of reinforcement means that the dog has no idea whether or not the behaviour will be rewarded. If you forget to take a treat with you when you go for a walk, it doesn't matter, though you should probably take something nice for him next time.

A reward or other form of reinforcement is not a bribe. You are not going to be luring your dog towards you in return for a treat. Using bribes does not result in a trained dog. Your recall will only be effectively trained when your dog does it despite not knowing if that particular time will result in a reward, and it is only effective when the dog will recall several times in a row, without receiving a reward at all. When you are using food rewards, they should be tucked away out of sight, in a bag or pocket, until after the successful recall has been completed.

Using jackpots

In addition to the power of random rewards, we are able to utilise yet another feature of the gambling effect. Rewards in nature are rarely all the same size. Sometimes an animal will get a very small reward, while on another occasion he will get a massive one... he has hit the jackpot! It is a good idea to incorporate this effect in your training, surprising your dog with an occasional jackpot or extra-large reward when he returns to you. Jackpots have a powerful training effect. Popular jackpot rewards with dogs are those little tins or pouches of luxury wet cat food. Open one up and let him have the whole thing. Dogs love them and you can put one in your pocket when you go for a walk to give him an occasional and more substantial treat. With really challenging dogs, you may need to go to even greater lengths with your jackpots and use some seriously generous treats such as a very large portion of hot roast chicken fresh from the carcass (don't give him the bones), or hot baked ham. These can often be purchased from your local supermarket and are useful in providing a high-value jackpot for dealing with serious recall problems. You can read more about this technique in *The Absconder* in Part Three.

What the gambling effect means for you is that once your dog is trained, the occasional treat will keep that training in place. You won't have to drag a trolley full of food everywhere for the next ten years.

Introducing non-food rewards

I recommend that you get your dog working well for food initially, simply because food is so convenient, portable and effective. You won't have to think about it, you can just pick up your treat bag and go. However, once your dog is working hard for food rewards, you can begin switching some of these for other rewards. Toys and games are rewarding to some dogs, but the key is working out what is rewarding to your dog.

Setting the dog up to win

Essentially, by using this training programme, you are making a conscious choice to always set the dog up to win. Punishment and reinforcement are both ways of diminishing or enhancing behaviours, but using punishment is difficult to apply accurately when a dog is not with you, and rewarding the dog is a much easier and more enjoyable way to teach your dog to run to you.

Through the application of carefully timed and scheduled rewards we can make dramatic changes in a dog's behaviour. Recall is an easy skill to reward effectively because every single successful recall culminates in the dog arriving in front of you. Your job is to repeatedly create situations in which the dog can succeed and be instantly rewarded for his success.

In the next chapter we look at how we can put this theory and knowledge to good use as we begin the process of permanently changing your dog's behaviour through practical reward-based training.

CHAPTER 4

Practical Training with Rewards

This chapter is about the practical application of some of the dog training theory we have looked at so far. In the previous chapter we looked at how the consequences of a dog's behaviour, including his response to your commands, can be controlled through the careful application of either punishments or rewards. We also noted that both of these types of consequence must be applied immediately after the dog's actions if they are to be effective enhancers or diminishers of behaviour.

I hope I have convinced you that, putting ethical arguments to one side, punishment is simply not a very practical method of behavioural modification when it comes to recall – both because of the difficulties of applying punishments in a timely manner during recall, and because a side effect of punishment is to reduce your dog's desire to be with you. For those reasons, this training programme is based on the use of rewards, and we have gone into some detail regarding the types of rewards you can use during training and the way in which rewards are applied.

In this chapter I will run through the five main stages of reward-based training. We will also be looking at the recall signal itself. Traditional training methods often involved giving a signal or command and then manoeuvring the dog into the right position. With modern reward-based training we don't begin with a command, we begin with a behaviour. Once the behaviour is established, we give it a name. There is sound logic behind this approach. Here are the five phases.

The five key components of training

This Recall Training Programme consists of five key components. They are as follows:

- Establishing the recall behaviour

- Associating the recall signal

- Obeying the recall signal

- Proofing the recall

- Maintaining the recall

Let's have a look at the third component, which is the point at which most people expect to start training. Obeying the recall signal is all about command recognition. This is where the dog recognises that the signal is a command, a call to action. Initially, this can seem like a logical place to start because using the signal or command is what most people associate with dog training. They want to give a command and have the dog respond to it promptly.

Obeying the recall signal

In order to teach the dog to respond to a signal without using punishments, we need to give the signal, then get the dog to carry out the behaviour, and then reward the dog. But the dog doesn't know what the signal means yet. He doesn't speak English or 'whistle'. You can't just blow a whistle for the first time and expect him to come back to you. Indeed, we don't want to use the whistle under these conditions because that would probably associate the whistle with something completely inappropriate, like standing still or tail wagging. So how do we get the dog to make those initial recall responses to the whistle in order to give him his reward and start generating a trained reaction to your signal?

What we need is a way to give the whistle some meaning, before we ever attempt to recall the dog. If the dog understood what the whistle meant, before we asked him to return when he hears it, that would be really helpful.

Learning through association

Scientists have observed a useful phenomenon, that repeated pairing of two unrelated events forms an important association between them, which is very useful to animal trainers. If we pair reward markers repeatedly with rewards, the markers themselves eventually take on some of the properties of the reward. That is to say the dog finds the marker itself quite rewarding to hear.

In a similar way we can build an association in the dog's brain between the recall signal and the act of moving towards his owner just by pairing the two. The more we pair the recall signal with the recall behaviour, the stronger this association becomes. So, in this part of our training, we focus on pairing together the whistle and the recall, over and over again, until a deep link is formed between them. Then when we need the dog to respond to the signal, the recall behaviour we have previously paired with it seems the natural thing to do.

Establishing the recall behaviour

Taking a step back now, to the very first of our five components, we need to know how, in practical terms, we are going to pair these two events – the recall and the recall whistle. How are we going to get the dog to move towards us, so that we can pair the recall signal with the recall behaviour? We can do that in two ways, either deliberately or opportunistically.

We can deliberately pair the recall with the whistle by luring, or otherwise encouraging, the dog towards us. This is particularly easy with puppies because they are naturally inclined to follow people and chase after them.

With older dogs, we can encourage the dog to come to us by attracting his attention and making lots of encouraging noises. We can run away from the dog, and if necessary we can attract him with food, toys, and so on. It doesn't matter that these are lures; this is just a temporary stage we need to go through to give us plenty of opportunities to pair together the recall and its signal.

We can also take advantages of any opportunities that the dog offers us to pair these two events. Any time your dog runs towards you of his own free will, for example, you can blow the recall whistle. This too will deepen the association between the recall behaviour and the recall signal.

Let's move forward to that third component again. When you get to this point, you will have established some recall behaviour. You will have got your puppy running after you by encouraging him to chase you, or your older dog to move towards you by backing away with his food bowl. You will have built an association between your recall signal and the recall behaviour by blowing it whenever your dog goes through the motions of heading in your direction. You will have then attempted to recall your dog in the house using your recall signal.

And it works! Your dog obeys the recall signal.

You blow the whistle, and your dog shoots across the room whereupon you make a huge fuss of him and give him some tasty treats. Not only that, he does it again, and again and again. Phew! At last, your dog understands the recall command.

Or does he?

Proofing the behaviour

This is the point in training where many dog owners go wrong. They take their dog, who has just begun to grasp the meaning of the recall command at home, into a public park or onto a beach where everything promptly falls apart. This is because they have not yet worked through the fourth component of recall training, proofing the behaviour.

The dog that is obeying the signal is still quite close to the beginning of the recall training process. He has only successfully completed a recall under very specific and highly controlled conditions. He does not yet know what the recall signal means in different situations.

Proofing means overcoming a dog's inability to generalise commands, and because proofing is so important, we will go into it in more detail in the next chapter. It is this phase in training that occupies the majority of the training programme.

Maintaining the behaviour

The fifth and final component of recall training carries on throughout the dog's life. Remember how trained responses are subject to extinction? We need to take active steps to maintain your great new recall, in order to prevent it becoming extinct. This is by far the easiest part of the training process but it does require a little thought and care on your part.

From time to time you will need to ask yourself:

- Am I rewarding my dog frequently enough?

- Am I using rewards that are valued by my dog?

- Am I taking opportunities to 'top up' his recall conditioning?

If your recall starts to get a little sloppy, a nice way to tighten it up is with the 'About Turn' walk in chapter twenty, but we will talk some more about maintaining a great recall at the end of the training programme.

Your recall signal

Before we move on to chapter five and look at the important process of proofing, we will talk about the recall signal itself. Before you can begin recall training you need to choose a brand new recall signal. You cannot work through the training programme using your tatty old recall command. This is crucial.

Old recall commands have old meanings and associations for your dog. Few of these meanings and associations have anything at all to do with recall and these old associations are hard to shake off. If your three-year-old dog has been trained to come to the signal 'Here Boy' then he is probably quite clear as to what 'Here Boy' means to him. It might mean 'We are nearly at the end of our walk now and I want you to come here in a minute or two so that you can't race around the car park getting in everyone's way'.

Or it might mean:

'If you don't come here after I have said "Here Boy" seven more times, I am going to shout COME HERE very loudly and go red in the face'.

You get the picture. These are not meanings that you want associated with your recall signal. So ditch the old one. We are starting afresh.

I recommend that all dogs be taught to recall to a plastic dog whistle. This is for a number of reasons:

- The whistle is consistent

- The whistle sound carries well

- Other people cannot easily interfere with your training

Whistles are completely unambiguous. The sound of the whistle is totally consistent and unlike your voice does not have the capacity to sound grumpy or irritable. If you are angry, or fed up, the whistle will not betray this fact in the way that subtle changes in your tone of voice do. It is also far easier for a dog to hear a whistle than your voice at a distance, especially in windy weather, and far more dignified than bellowing to a dog that is two hundred yards away.

An additional benefit of the whistle is that it prevents other people from interfering with the training process or recalling the dog without you knowing. Good recall conditioning is impossible if other family members pair the recall signal repeatedly with all kinds of inappropriate behaviour. And changes in behaviour are unlikely to be the ones you desire if the consequences of the dog's actions are not controlled after the recall signal has been given. This kind of interference can be a real problem in some families, where the person training the dog has to struggle against other family members who busily undo all their training.

With a whistle, you can keep it safely put away and make sure that it is only used under your supervision.

The only disadvantage to your whistle is that you need to remember to take it with you, but I think that this is a small price to pay for the many advantages.

Before you start training I recommend that you buy two Acme Gundog Whistles, either a 210.5 or 211.5 pitch. These whistles are made from strong hard plastic and the pitch never varies. They are ideal for any breed of dog and if you lose your Acme whistle, you can replace it with another of the same pitch, which will sound exactly the same. Your dog will never know the difference. You will also need a lanyard to hang your whistle around your neck. Acme gundog whistles can be purchased online or in many gun shops.

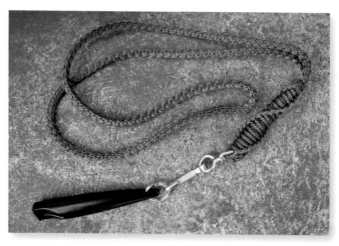

You will need a lanyard to hang your whistle around your neck

Don't use a stag's horn whistle as they all sound different and you will lose yours at some point. Once you have bought your whistle, practise blowing it where your dog cannot hear it until you have perfected your signal.

A typical whistle recall is a string of pips, like this 'pip-pip-pip' or 'pip-pip-pip-pip-pip'. I use five pips to clearly distinguish a recall from a turn whistle (two pips), but if you are not intending to get involved in gundog work, there is no reason why you shouldn't use a different number of pips. Just decide on the signal and stick to it.

Once you have completed the training programme, if you want to teach your dog to come to a verbal command for those times when he is close by or indoors, then by all means do so. Dogs are quite capable of learning more than one recall signal.

Once you have bought your whistle you are nearly ready to start working through the five phases in reward-based recall training. But before we start, let's just have a look at the most important part of an effective dog training programme, and at the key factors which can influence your ability to complete this process with style! Let's look at proofing.

CHAPTER 5

All About Proofing

We looked in the previous chapter at the five phases of training. Without doubt, the phase that most people have trouble with is proofing. Many pet dog owners are unaware that proofing exists, let alone how important it is. They simply expect that a whistle obeyed in the garden should be obeyed on the beach.

A common complaint from many dog owners is that their dog knows perfectly well what 'Come here' means, but that he fails to obey them when there are other dogs, or people, about. We now know that the concept of deliberate disobedience is flawed when it comes to dogs. It is highly unlikely that any dog is capable of mulling over his options.

A dog does not think to himself 'Hmm, she has blown the recall whistle, but I really want to go and say hello to that nice Labrador over there, so she will just have to wait for a minute.'

He is not 'choosing' to be disobedient, however tempting it may be to make this assumption. Recall is simply a trained response to a cue. In this case the cue is the whistle. If the dog does not respond to the whistle, in most cases it is because the owner failed to effectively train the dog to respond in that kind of situation. The whistle simply means nothing to him in this context because his training has not been 'proofed'. But what exactly is this proofing process and why is it so important?

What is proofing?

Proofing is the bit where you teach the dog that the action he carries out when we give a signal, such as a whistle or command word, must be carried out under all manner of circumstances.

This is the part many books skim over or ignore, and which is impossible to address in the confines of an indoor training class. It is the longest stage in training and the most neglected. Many people don't even attempt proofing at all and feel incredibly frustrated and confused when their dog refuses to recall in a public place. 'He's ever so good at home,' they say, or 'He knows he's being bad, he even looks guilty when I tell him off'.

Some families evolve interesting and complex routines to manage their dog's lack of proofing, often involving exercising him at highly unsocial hours to avoid contact with other people. Others are reduced to keeping the dog permanently on some kind of expanding lead. That is not a road you want to go down. Proofing takes a bit of time and effort but it is what stands between you and a really reliable recall, so it is well worth getting on with it.

Why is proofing necessary?

As we have seen, dogs do not generalise very well. They find it difficult to understand that a command that they have learned to obey in one location, under one set of conditions, also applies in other locations and under different conditions.

This means that initially you must train the response you require under a wide range of circumstances. Gradually, over time, the dog becomes better at generalising the command. Give the dog so many opportunities to experience the sound of the recall signal whilst he is racing towards you that it becomes a deeply ingrained habit. Once he has recalled in many different places and under lots of different conditions, the recall response becomes virtually automatic and will then be effective in new locations and under new conditions. But this process takes time, and individual dogs vary in the amount of proofing that is necessary for them to understand that the recall always means the same, no matter when or where it occurs.

Are there alternatives to proofing?

Traditional, dog trainers used a 'challenge' method of overcoming a dog's inability to generalise. The dog would be taught the basic command at home, without distractions, as we do in this programme. He would then be taken to different locations and exposed to different distractions, to challenge his obedience. In other words, the dog would be set up to fail. The idea was that the failure would occur in a controlled situation so the trainer could then punish the dog in a timely and effective manner, and the dog would be less likely to repeat the behaviour in the future. However, as we have touched on previously, accurately applying punishment to a failed recall is often problematical.

Whilst in a few specific situations there may be a place for the challenge method, it can be pretty tough on the dog and his owner. Modern proofing gets good results without the adverse effects of regular and unpleasant punishments, and is gradually taking over from challenge methods in most dog training activities and sport.

What does proofing involve?

Proofing involves the repetitive retraining of a response to a signal under lots of different conditions. It involves setting up 'fake' scenarios where you control the introduction of the kinds of distractions that might otherwise cause your dog to fail to respond to your recall signal. You will find lots of these fake set-ups in the training programme. They enable you to put the dog into a distracting situation in such a way that you have control over all the factors or variables that might influence him, and can maximise the chances of him succeeding and deepening his good recall habit.

You'll notice that in the training section we begin our proofing exercises by introducing other people and dogs into your recall at home.

If you cannot recall your dog away from an interesting visitor in your back garden, you stand no chance of being able to recall him away from a fascinating stranger on a footpath in the middle of a sixty-acre field. To get from a simple recall in your garden to a challenging one outdoors, we need to build up the recall in stages. And each of these stages deals with specific distractions.

The power of distractions

What we refer to as distractions includes a wide range of factors. A change in location is highly distracting to most young dogs. Next time you get your dog out of the car at a new location, keep him on the lead next to the car for a moment and observe him. His attention will be all over the place, tail wagging, sniffing the air, ears up with anticipation. The thought of exploring all this 'new stuff' is extremely exciting to many dogs. For this reason alone, recalling your dog in the park where he is familiar with his surroundings is not the same as recalling him in a forest where he has never been.

Strong scent is also a powerful distraction to training. Teaching a dog on a bare and uninteresting surface, such as your driveway or lawn, is a very different matter from teaching him on a field covered with the scent trails of the rabbits that were feeding there during the night. Anything new or different can be very distracting, including changes in terrain. Wet mud is different from heather, for example, and water in small or large quantities is a powerful distraction to many dogs. Even changes in the weather are distracting.

You are probably already aware of the distracting power of other animals. Squirrels, butterflies, cats and rabbits all pose problems for the dog trainer, and for many sociable dogs, one of the most powerful distractions is the presence of other dogs.

Every recall is unique

Recalling a dog is not a standardised event. No two recalls are ever exactly the same. In addition to the presence of the distractions just discussed, there are many, many other factors of difficulty that can be added to a recall. A factor such as how far away from you your dog is when you call him is important. The proximity and activity levels of distractions matter, too. A strange dog sitting quietly by its owner is less attractive to your dog than one walking along at heel, which is less attractive still than a dog that is rushing about or playing with a ball.

Proofing in stages involves introducing factors one at a time, one level at a time, beginning with the least distracting and working your way up.

The challenges of proofing

Proofing is challenging because each new distraction we expose the dog to reintroduces the possibility that he will fail to obey the recall. In addition, each new distraction introduces fresh challenges when it comes to preventing your dog from self-rewarding. Remember that anything the dog is choosing to do rather than come to you can reasonably be construed as self-rewarding.

More than just training

Of course your 'appeal', as far as the dog is concerned, is a key factor in triggering recall behaviour and in avoiding problems. Another factor is the opportunities you give your dog to self-reward during your walks together. This is why recall training is about more than just training – it is also about the way you relate to your dog and the way you manage his options. We will be looking more closely at this in the next chapter.

Is it all too much?

Sometimes a dog owner will be horrified at what is actually required to proof their training effectively, wondering how they can possibly be expected to go to all that trouble.

But please don't panic! The proofing process is really all about gathering new experiences for your dog and can actually be a lot of fun. It is a great excuse to get out and about in different places with your dog, and you will be planning ahead to avoid any nasty surprises and to enable your dog to learn to recall successfully in increasingly challenging environments.

I won't be asking you to take your dog to places that you wouldn't dream of taking him otherwise, or to get involved in situations that you would never normally contemplate. The idea is to get your dog to recall effortlessly in the places, and under the conditions, that you will be likely to take him to in the future.

Don't forget that even if you paid no attention to proofing, you would still end up in many of the situations we set up for you in the programme. However, this way you get to control the outcome and with every success-ful recall we set up, your new recall signal grows stronger.

The rewards of proofing

Proofing gets results. It teaches your dog to respond to your recall com-mand anywhere and at any time (within reason). With proofing you get what you train for and sometimes more. As you teach your dog to come to you in an increasing number of locations, and among more and more distractions, you eventually get to the point where the recall response is automatic and will work even in situations that you haven't trained for. Best of all, proofing is a humane and kindly way to establish a reliable trained response in any dog.

Decades of harsh treatment towards dogs is, for the most part, a result of simple misunderstanding. This behaviour was based on the mistaken belief that dogs were being deliberately naughty, when in fact they were just inadequately trained. Thanks to modern proofing methods we will never need to go down this route again.

Perhaps the greatest challenge lies in devising the situations you require in order to proof your dog's recall under a wide range of con-ditions. To save your brain from melting, I have provided a number of proofing exercises within the training programme – all you need to do is work through each one with your dog. If you think of more examples that fit in with your lifestyle then by all means add them on. The more you practise, the better your recall will become.

Life goes on during proofing

Because proofing takes time, and effectively adds that time on to the training process, you might wonder if your life is going to be put on hold for the next few months. Don't worry. Unless your dog has serious problems you will still be able to take him out and about with you. You do not need to wait until proofing is complete before you take him out in public, you just need to take some precautions to avoid spoiling your dog's nice new, but still fragile, recall habits. The most important precaution is to avoid using your new recall in situations you haven't yet trained for, or in any situation where you think the dog may not come. This means being a little bit selective. If you want your dog and he is a hundred yards away, unless you have taught him to come from a hundred yards away, don't call him. Try running away from him to get him to chase you, or walk a lot closer and call him from a distance you know he can achieve.

Be very picky about using your new recall – for the next few months it is delicate and easily crushed. As you work through the proofing process it will grow steadily stronger.

CHAPTER **6**

Beyond Training

There are a number of factors that can influence your ability to train your dog, especially during the proofing process. They are as follows:

- The temperament of the dog
- Past experiences the dog has had
- The way you manage and supervise the dog
- The way you interact with the dog

These factors act together, as well as individually, to influence the value your dog places on your company. This profoundly affects your ability to achieve an effective and reliable recall.

The temperament of the dog

Generations of selective breeding, for characteristics that human beings find attractive or useful, has created a huge diversity in canine form.

Dogs vary widely, not only in appearance but in temperament, too. Some dogs have been bred to be highly cooperative in order to work closely with human beings. Herding dogs and retrievers are examples of highly sociable and cooperative dogs. Some breeds have been bred to work almost entirely independently from human beings, and these dogs have developed a much looser relationship with people based on exchange of resources, food, somewhere dry to sleep and so on. Hounds, sled dogs and terriers are often classified as 'difficult to train' or 'wilful'. They are not particularly influenced by human approval and may be very resistant to forceful training techniques.

Another character trait that can cause problems for dog owners is a set of powerful hunting or chasing instincts. Dogs that are easily excited by the scent or sight of wild animals will find it very easy to self-reward in the countryside. Problems with dogs from gundog breeds that have very strong hunting and chasing instincts are common – including working strains of some of the hunting breeds of gundog such as the English Springer Spaniel. People often expect a high level of cooperation from a gundog and are not prepared when they find themselves in trouble.

Dogs that are highly excited by moving objects, or by other dogs, may find it very easy to self-reward in a park or on a busy beach. This can pose an extra challenge for the trainer when he attempts to control consequences outdoors.

When these two attributes (chasing instincts and lack of desire to cooperate) come together as they do in some of the sight hound breeds, you may have a particularly challenging dog on your hands. Fortunately, effective reward-based training helps to create a more level playing field. But an effective management system is also essential if you are to complete your training successfully, and we will talk about that in a minute.

Past experiences

Some dogs have a chequered past when it comes to recall. Many will have developed bad habits and will have collected a wealth of amazingly rewarding experiences whilst gallivanting around the countryside, ignoring the pleas of their owners. These experiences may have led the dog to believe that people in general, and you in particular, have nothing remotely interesting to offer him in comparison with the pleasures he can get for himself. This kind of history is apparent in some adopted or rescued dogs.

Giving a home and a new chance to a rescue dog is highly rewarding and satisfying. But it is important to be aware that some rescue dogs will have recall issues that need to be addressed through proper management and retraining. Part of the reason for this is that it takes time for an adult dog to fully bond with, and want to be with, his new family. It is also because dogs with recall problems are more likely to end up being abandoned in the first place.

Remember that whatever your dog's history or temperament, success in training the recall is dependent on you controlling the consequences of your dog's behaviour. This may be more challenging with some dogs than others, but is nearly always achievable.

Although you have no control over your dog's history, or the genes he has inherited, it does help to recognise these attributes. This will enable you to work on changing your dog's attitude towards you and to manage your unique dog appropriately to reduce the chances of him gaining a reward in the future without your permission. Which leads us to the question of supervision.

Supervising your dog

British dog owners love their daily walks. Our nation is criss-crossed with a network of footpaths and, unless you live in a city centre, the chances are you will be walking your dog off-lead regularly, on public footpaths through fields, parks or woods. Many dog walkers drive into the country-side to popular dog walking locations. They park up, tip the dog out of the car and let him go, without much thought about what he is up to or how he is affecting the wildlife or other walkers and their dogs. While some dogs come to no harm with this approach, releasing a dog into the coun-tryside and leaving him to his own devices, while you relax and enjoy the view or chat to friends, is not a good strategy with a young dog – especially a dog from hunting or working lines. This reactive approach (leaving him to entertain himself until he gets into trouble) will often end in misery as the dog will learn to provide his own amusement and build up a repertoire of bad habits.

For this reason, as well as for his safety, it is important to manage and supervise your dog's off-lead exercise, and the best way to do that is through interaction. If your dog is busy working or playing with you, then he is not getting into mischief.

Interacting with your dog

All successful trainers of active dogs have two things in common – they control the rewards and they interact with their dogs.

Think about what your dog finds most rewarding. For many dogs it will be free running exercise and dinner time. Think about how your dog gets these things. The chances are that when you go for a walk you take off his lead ONCE. That is one reward for your dog. One point for you. Your dog on the other hand gives himself a great many rewards during the course of a walk. He chases a butterfly, greets other dogs, sticks his head down rabbit holes, rolls in something delectable, and much more. He probably gets himself a dozen or more rewards during the course of a half-hour walk. That is twelve points for your dog.

And what about dinner time? Most people feed adult dogs once or twice a day. Two points for you. You are not doing very well so far. Three points for you and twelve for your dog. Your dog can safely conclude that he is better off looking for his own rewards than relying on you to provide them.

So how can you turn this situation on its head? How can you become more interesting and more valuable to your dog? The answer is to engage in activities with your dog during the course of your daily walks. These activities can include training sessions, tracking games, retrieving and so on. This will give you lots of opportunities to reward your dog and to keep him mentally stimulated.

Managed exercise

Dogs prefer to be where the action is. If you think about how most people behave when they walk their dogs, plodding along in a straight line, you get an idea of just how dull, predictable and unappealing they are to a young and boisterous dog. With managed exercise the idea is to divide the walk into sections and to intersperse periods of free running with periods of training and games. This serves a number of purposes:

- It gives you numerous opportunities to reward the dog
- It makes you more interesting to be around
- It helps to keep the dog close

If you release your dog from his lead ten times during a walk, you have given him ten rewards. This is very important. Letting the dog go just once at the beginning of a walk is to deny yourself a great many opportunities to give him his favourite reward... free running.

Games and activities

Involving your dog in games and activities can transform the way he sees you. One great way to amuse dogs is with retrieving games. Half of all dogs in the UK are gundog types and these breeds will often retrieve naturally and without much encouragement. Many other dogs will also readily retrieve, and those that won't can be taught to do so. If your dog enjoys retrieving a ball, Frisbee or toy, you have a fantastic tool for entertaining and amusing him.

Any walk can be made more interesting with 'go-back retrieves'. You simply walk along with your dog at heel and drop a ball or dummy to one side of the path where he can clearly see it. Walk on a few paces and then send him back for it. Dogs love this game. You can build up to longer and longer distances as your dog's memory and skill improves. Retrieving is simply the best way to allow your dog off-leash exercise without losing control. You can find out more about retrieving on my gundog website www.totallygundogs.com.

Ball games are a great way of entertaining a dog

Some dogs will enjoy stopping for a game of tug. A good game to start when your dog is quite young and not yet fully independent is hide and seek; just wait until your dog is busy investigating a leaf or an interesting bush that another dog has peed on and slip behind a tree. Watch your dog puzzle out where you are using his nose to track your footsteps. Obviously this game requires some common sense; if your dog doesn't find you quite quickly, don't wait until he is in a complete panic before revealing yourself, and don't do this with a small puppy.

Remember that dogs are easily bored and actively seek out excitement and interesting things to do. If you fail to provide that excitement or those interesting things, you can't blame your dog for looking elsewhere for his fun.

The zone of control

Don't wait until things are going badly wrong before deciding to manage your walks more effectively. Take action before problems arise. The dogs that will benefit most from a policy of supervision and control during walks are ones that are:

- Overly confident at a young age

- Uninterested in you when outdoors

- Spending longer and longer out of your sight during walks

- Showing signs of strong chasing or hunting behaviour

Your first task with any of these dogs is to establish a 'zone of control': a range or circle around you, outside of which your dog is not allowed to stray. Use the games and activities we have discussed to keep your dog focused on you, and to encourage him back to you whenever he reaches the edge of the zone. Some dogs will need to wear a training lead while you establish the zone. This is a long line that trails behind the dog, and which you can use to prevent him from going too far away. You can read up on using a training lead in Part Three.

Remember, a dog should not be out of your sight for long periods of time. A dog does not have to go far to find exciting birds, deer, sheep or rabbits to chase to his heart's content. Nor will he need to chase far before he finds a road to cross. Not only is he a risk to himself, and a nuisance to others, he will have countless opportunities for rewarding himself. His rewards need to come from you.

Don't forget to break your walk into different sections. For example, five minutes walking with the dog running free in the zone of control, five minutes training or games, five minutes with the dog walking along at heel, and then five more minutes free running in the zone, and so on. The walking to heel part benefits you both – it allows you both to switch off and relax. You can chat to friends or simply enjoy the view without worrying about your dog. There is no need for any dog to run free for the entire duration of a walk, and if you if let him do this at the same time as supervising him within your zone, you will fry your brain.

Give yourself a break and put the dog on a lead for five minutes.

Spotting trouble

Often, when a dog gets himself into trouble, the situation could have been avoided by some crafty behaviour on the part of the owner. You need to be alert when managing your dog outdoors, and learn to spot trouble in advance. Your ability to do this is greatly facilitated by a policy of keeping the dog in the zone of control.

If your dog is close to you, you will be able to spot the first signs of an impending chase and intervene. A dog will often pause or freeze before setting off. He may even turn to look at you as if to say, 'let's get it!'. Now is your cue to interrupt his intentions with a firm 'NO!' followed by a strong recall (run away from the dog to switch his chasing instinct on to you).

If this does not work and your dog gives chase, do not keep calling him. Repeated recall during chase activities does huge damage to your recall command because it builds an unwanted association between recall and running away. Never call a dog in full flight unless you have trained him to recall under these conditions. He won't stop and you will spoil your recall. Next time you take him into the same situation, make sure he is on a training lead so you can prevent him from rewarding himself for ignoring you.

Just like us, dogs get bored and are happiest when occupied. Why not enrol your dog in agility classes, or have a go at working trials, or CaniX. If you own a gundog, take him gundog training. There is information about these and other activities at the end of this book.

Everything a dog needs to build a solid relationship with his owner is based on mutual respect, interaction and activity. It is impossible to over-state the value of activity to most dogs. If you can dramatically multiply the number of times you release your dog each time you walk together, you will raise your value in his eyes. It is not possible to build this kind of relationship with a dog that you only catch brief glimpses of during a three-mile walk. Remember, if you do not know where your dog is, and what he is doing, it is probably best to assume that he is up to no good.

Combining good training and management

Getting a dog to come back when he is called, every time he is called, requires a combination of effective training and sensible management of his access to free running off-lead exercise. These two factors (training and management) interact and influence each other throughout a dog's life. The better a dog is managed, the less effect a few slip-ups in training will have. And the more thorough the dog's recall training has been, the less effect there will be from any shortcomings in managing the dog.

The way in which you interact with your dog on a daily basis, and particularly the way in which you interact with him during his outdoor off-lead exercise, has a profound effect on the relationship between the two of you. Your dog could be the cleverest on the planet, or a complete fool; he could have the patience of a saint or the attention span of a gnat; it does not matter. You can make a success of your training provided you remain valuable and interesting to your dog.

CHAPTER 7

Your Dog

As you can see, recall is more than a simple training issue. How you approach your recall training, including the other steps you take to resolve any recall problems, will depend on your dog, his age, his temperament and his past history. We need to consider the whole dog before we start trying to train him.

Think about your starting point before you begin. Is your dog:

- A puppy under five months old

- An older dog with no serious problems

- Somewhat out of control

- A serious absconder

Starting with a puppy

Starting this recall training programme with a young puppy provides you with a unique opportunity to avoid the mistakes that so many people make with managing their first dog. Especially when it comes to exercising a dog out in the countryside.

Achieving an excellent recall from scratch requires a structured approach to training. And that is what Part Two of this book is for. But before you begin training, do think about how you plan to supervise and manage your puppy outdoors, as he grows and becomes more confident. Find out as much as you can about the natural characteristics of your puppy's breed. If he belongs to one of the more challenging breeds, it is very important that you pay extra attention to building a strong relationship with your dog.

Make sure you are interesting to your puppy. One very simple way to be more interesting to your dog during your walks together is to be unpredictable, so when you first start taking your puppy out on walks try to avoid endlessly plodding along the same old path – change direction often. By that I mean literally turn around on the spot and start walking back the way you came. You cannot do this too much. Puppies less than six months old lack the confidence to lead the way and are inclined to follow you. Make the most of this to establish a firm habit in your dog, of watching you to see where you go next. This helps your dog to see you as the person who leads rather than the person who follows. Remember that pups do not need long walks, just five minutes or so per day for each month of their age. Half an hour a day is enough for a six-month-old dog.

Make sure that you review your assessment of your puppy as he matures. Try to be objective and to take avoiding action if you start to feel out of control at any point.

An older dog with no serious problems

If your older dog's recall is simply a little sloppy, you may find that working through the *About Turn Walk* in Part Three, using your existing recall command, is sufficient training for your current needs. However, many adult dogs will benefit from a thorough retraining of the recall, working through the training programme in Part Two using a brand new recall signal. If your dog's old recall still works after a fashion, you can save the new one for emergencies, provided that you regularly condition it by using the signal whenever your dog returns to you voluntarily, and following it up with a great reward. You can use both approaches in parallel as long as you remember to safeguard your new recall signal and never use it, except in a dire emergency, unless success is guaranteed.

A dog with control issues

If your dog regularly ignores your recall command and comes back in his own good time, not yours; if he often chases other animals on walks, and you sometimes worry for his safety; if you find you are not enjoying walks and sometimes make excuses not to go, you probably have control issues. If you feel like you are losing control, then you probably are! You might find it helpful to read chapter eighteen, *Out of Control?*.

Now is the time to make a fresh start and thoroughly train a brand-new recall that puts you back in the driving seat. However, the keen hunting dog requires some additional effort. Not only will you need to work through the training programme in exactly the same way as you would with any other dog, you will also need to give some extra consideration to how you are going to manage his free time. You cannot just go back to what you were doing before. If you don't give this subject some serious consideration, your ability to control the proofing process will be seriously impaired. This is because much of the training process is dependent on controlling all high-value rewards available to the dog, and for a keen hunting dog the reward with the highest value is often hunting itself. If your dog has been galloping across the length and breadth of the county chasing rabbits and deer for the last three months, you are going to have to make some profound changes to the way you manage his exercise in order for your new recall training to stand a chance.

The information on managed exercise in the previous chapter is especially relevant to you and your dog, and you need to begin working through the Recall Training Programme using a brand new recall command. You may find engaging in some further activities with your dog useful, and there is more information about this in the final chapter of this book. I especially recommend that you teach your dog to retrieve if he doesn't already. This is because retrieving is a brilliant way of giving off-lead exercise to a dog in a controlled manner.

Do have a read through the chapter entitled *Using a Training Lead* as you will almost certainly need to take advantage of this helpful piece of equipment during the training programme.

The serious absconder

With recall it is never too late, and things are never so bad that they cannot be improved.

But of course, the more serious and deeply ingrained your dog's bad habits, the longer it will take to achieve a real and permanent cure. The serial absconder is a big worry for his owners. He just takes off when let off the lead and sometimes does not return for hours. If things are getting serious and your dog is now completely out of control for much of your walk, if you are worried for his safety and cannot recall him with any certainty until he is ready to go home, then you will need to stop allowing the dog to run around off lead, while you work through the Recall Training Programme in Part Two. In the meantime, you will need to lead-walk your dog and find an enclosed space to let him have some regular free-running exercise until you are ready to reintroduce him to your outdoor locations, as part of the training programme.

For dogs with a history of running away you will need to use a training lead for some considerable time outdoors. You will find more information in chapter nineteen, *The Absconder*.

This kind of recall problem is curable but it may take many months and you will need to be extremely committed to see it through.

Building great habits

Good training is about forming good habits. Patterns of behaviour form well-used paths in our brains as well as in the brains of our dogs. If you walk the same walk each day, if you do your chores in the same order, get up at the same time, eat the same food, these things become habit. It is easier by far to do them in the same habitual way than it is to do them differently. A trained response is also a habit, a well-worn path, and the more times we pass along the path, the harder it is to stray from it.

Whatever your starting point, our destinations are the same. We all want a dog that comes when he is called, every time he is called, no matter what he is doing. Let's have a look now at some of the strategies that will help us to achieve our goal.

CHAPTER 8

Are You Ready?

Throughout the training programme we will be using strategies that build confidence in the dog and trust in his handler, you. We will be teaching your dog that you are the centre of his world, the source of all that is fun and enjoyable, and that the best (and only) way to get what he wants is to come when you call him.

Let's review our basic training strategies and take a peek at what is inside the training programme.

The training programme

The training programme is divided into stages. There are suggestions in some of the chapters for extra practice and background information relevant to that particular stage in training. At the end of each training chapter are some questions, and you should be able to answer yes to each of these before moving on to the next chapter.

Each chapter in the programme contains a number of exercises. Work through each exercise until your dog is able to complete the recall easily and without extra encouragement or help from you.

In each exercise the recall command is given just once. The objective is for the dog to rush to you immediately when he hears the whistle. Remember, do not repeat the signal.

If the dog does not come immediately, you must take action to ensure that he completes the recall and is not rewarded in any other way until he does so.

If the dog fails to respond to the recall signal you will:

- Prevent self-rewarding

- Initiate the recall

- Give higher value rewards when successful

Each exercise is set up to help you prevent the dog from rewarding himself. The idea is to show the dog that the best possible outcome he can achieve is to come to you.

The training strategies

To increase our chances of success we need to make use of a number of key training strategies. Each of these strategies is based firmly on the sound research and experience of thousands of effective modern dog trainers working with reward-based training techniques. They should, by now, be familiar to you, but if in doubt do not hesitate to review the material in the preceding chapters for a full explanation. Here are the strategies you will need to keep you on the right track:

1. Start with a new signal

2. Set the dog up to win

3. Proof thoroughly

4. Give the signal only once

5. Use rewards effectively

6. Avoid repeating mistakes

7. Never punish a recall

8. Prevent self-rewarding

9. Accept your dog's limitations

10. Motivate yourself

The last strategy is about you, because without your involvement and commitment your dog can never fulfil his real potential.

We have talked a lot about rewards, let's have a quick review of the practical aspects of rewarding your dog that you need to remember before you jump into your first training session.

Practical use of rewards

Every time we introduce new challenges for the dog, we need to start with high-value rewards. This gives us the best chance of establishing the correct behaviour right from the start.

But what exactly do I mean by high value? I have divided your rewards into four different categories:

- Basic

- Premium

- Bonus

- Mega

Basic

Basic staple treats are very small (not much more than pea-sized). Little cubes of toast or cheese (mix together for cheese-flavoured toast), cubes of liver cake, even kibble will suffice for some dogs. By the end of the training programme, a few basic rewards are all that you will need to have with you on most occasions.

Premium

Think quality and moist. Premium treats are still small, though not tiny, and much tastier. More attractive food is often moist and smells inviting. Juicy half-inch chunks of roast chicken or beef make great premium treats. You will be using premium rewards a great deal in the early stages of training, because they help to speed up and cement the all important early responses to your new recall signal. With some dogs you will simply not get a training response established with anything less.

Think juicy! Premium rewards help to speed up and cement early responses

Bonus

Think quality, quantity and time. Bonus rewards are ultra-generous helpings of premium reward. Handfuls of roast chicken chunks, an entire pouch of tasty premium cat food, or a tin of sardines all make good bonus rewards, though the latter are very messy. The trick with the bonus is to string out the experience as long as you can and to feed from your hands. You will feed the dog continuously over a period of twenty to thirty seconds, breaking of little bits one after another to keep the experience going for him. Bonus rewards are what you use to give the dog an unexpected jackpot reward. We also use bonus rewards when we teach a new and difficult skill.

Mega

For many dogs you will not need to use 'mega' rewards, but for dogs with serious recall problems mega rewards are essential. A mega reward needs to 'blow your dog's mind'. Think quality, quantity, then even more quality. Warm is good because it smells much more appetising. Big chunks of hot roast chicken or gammon fresh from the oven (keep warm wrapped in a few layers of foil) make a great mega reward. Leave the fat and skin on and make sure it is dripping with juices and flavour.

What about jackpots?

A jackpot is simply an unexpected and unpredictable bonus reward. We use jackpots to deepen and maintain an established, trained response.

In each of the exercises in the training programme I indicate which type of rewards to use. Once we have a perfect response in a given situation, the value, quantity and frequency of rewards can be gradually reduced.

Switching from one level of reward to another

Each new level of difficulty will be accompanied by a return to higher-value reward, so do keep plenty of suitable rewards to hand. I appreciate that premium rewards are more expensive to provide than some basic rewards, especially if you buy pre-cooked roast meat, but the results are worth it. Remember that you get out what you put in.

What about different types of reward

As you progress through the training programme you will be incorporating more non-food rewards into your training exercises. These will include opportunities for your dog to indulge in behaviour that appeals to him such as playing with other dogs, chasing a ball or being stroked by strangers. You will need to consider your own dog's preferences when deciding how much emphasis to put on these types of rewards.

Ensuring success

Throughout the training exercises, each time you give a recall signal, we will be ensuring that the dog completes his recall. In some cases this will take time and effort but you should not give up, and certainly don't repeat the recall signal.

In each exercise, once the signal has been given you will be doing whatever it takes to get the dog to you. Here are some of the best ways to get a dog to run towards you:

- Run away from the dog

- Crouch down low with arms wide and welcoming

- Make lots of squeaky high-pitched encouraging noises

- Use the reward marker to let the dog know when he moves in the right direction

- Give masses of praise and encouragement as the dog moves towards you

Always try running away first as many dogs have a chase reflex well into adulthood and cannot resist pursuing you. Crouching down is great for sensitive dogs as it makes you completely unthreatening and very appealing. And while you may feel a bit silly squeaking and praising your dog in public, it often works.

We will introduce a reward marker to your dog from the start of the programme, and associate the marker with food. Later on we will be able to use the marker to let the dog know he is on the right track if he is struggling to complete an exercise.

Once you have achieved a successful recall in each exercise, provided you ensure that the dog cannot self-reward after the whistle signal, you will find the dog will get faster as you practise. You can speed up this process by selectively rewarding the fastest recalls and by taking every opportunity to build a strong association between your new signal and the fast recall behaviour that you desire.

Use the power of conditioning

In chapter four, *Practical Training with Rewards*, we talked about the power of conditioning or associating your signal with the desired behaviour, for giving your brand-new recall signal some meaning for your dog. Conditioning is so important that we will continue to take plenty of opportunities to make use of it throughout the training process and beyond.

This means taking advantage of any opportunities that your dog freely presents you with to use the whistle as he races towards you. This could be in the house or out on a walk, it doesn't matter which.

Taking the dog out during the programme

Unlike owners of a new puppy, those of you who have an older dog will probably be in the habit of taking him out and about in public, and will want to continue this habit during the training programme. If this applies to you, make sure you do not use your new recall command (the one you choose for this training programme) while you are out and about on your walks, not until you reach the relevant point in the training programme.

You must not use the new recall unless you set yourself up for success. Never use your new recall to get your dog back to you in situations that you have not trained for. If you are not training today, or in this location, leave your whistle at home. That way you won't add your new recall to the 'scrap heap' along with your old one.

Do check out the information on managed exercise in chapter six, it has the potential to transform your relationship with your dog. If you are still using your old recall on walks do try the About Turn Walk, it's a great way to tighten up a sloppy recall using your existing command. Also try to remember to mix difficult recalls in with lots of easy ones. This way if your dog does make a mistake, it will be one small error in a sea of success.

During the training programme try to avoid taking the older dog to places where you know he may get into trouble, or where you may be tempted to test out your new whistle signal before your dog is ready. Don't worry if this means his exercise is temporarily reduced a little. This will do him less harm in the long term than a poor or absent recall.

Remember, take care not to blow the whistle at any other time apart from during a voluntary recall initially, or when carrying out the exercises in the training programme. We do not want your nice shiny new signal to become associated inappropriately with some other behaviour – like chasing squirrels, stopping for a pee or sniffing a cat's bottom.

If you have had a lot of problems with your dog out and about in the countryside, you will find it helpful to read chapter seventeen, *Where Did I Go Wrong?*, and chapter eighteen, *Out of Control?*. If your dog has been running away, you need to read chapter nineteen, *The Absconder*, before you start training.

Remember not to punish the recall

No one intentionally punishes a recall, but it is important to make sure that you don't do this by mistake. Never call your dog with your brand-new recall and then follow it up with something he views as unpleasant. If you need to shut your dog away or take him home, just go and get him if you can.

If you can't simply get the dog, recall him and give him a fantastic reward, and then play with him for a few minutes before shutting him away so that he doesn't associate your recall with his fun being spoiled.

Working with a friend

Training a dog effectively always involves other people and other dogs. Many of us like training our dogs alone, and if you are one of those people, I sympathise. But the fact remains that all of the scenarios where your dog is most likely to be disobedient involve the presence of a third party, be it another animal or a person. Dogs don't disobey in a vacuum, they do so in response to distractions from around them. The only way to proof your training against these distractions is to set these very same distractions up in controlled conditions. This means getting help from friends, relatives and anyone you can rope in to assist you. You will also need a few sessions of help from a friend with a reasonably behaved dog or, if that is not an option, a dog trainer to help you with some parts of this programme.

It can be very helpful to work through the training programme with a friend. You will not be able to train together in the early stages, but as you work through the exercises you will be able to act as assistants for each other, and will have a good understanding of each other's needs.

Motivate your dog

All mammals need a motive in order to take action. Dogs need motivating. Don't expect something for nothing. Old-fashioned trainers often told us that dogs' behaviour was based on loyalty, respect or love. This simply is not true and all trainers that refuse to use rewards in training have to use the alternative – punishment – at some point. As we have seen, punishing a failed recall is very difficult task, almost all trainers my age or older will have tried it and often found it wanting. Motivation through rewards is the key to a great recall, so please do not be tempted to pay attention to people who tell you that food is cheating, or that it does not work. Set your dog up to win, and keep training. You will get there.

Motivate yourself

We have talked a lot about keeping your dog happy and successful, but unless we can do the same for you, this training won't happen. We all lead busy lives and there will always be something more important to do in your day than training the dog. If you fly into your dog training programme with too much intensity you may find you 'burn out' and resent the commitment quite quickly.

I recommend you start small and focus on getting a training habit established. Three or four minutes, three or four times a day, will have you and your dog enjoying each session and looking forward to the next one. If that is too much for you, a couple of minutes once or twice a day is a good start. The key is a daily commitment. It takes from thirty to sixty days to build a habit. Until the habit is established we have to make a conscious effort to do it. This is when the habit is most vulnerable.

Once a habit is established we no longer have to think hard about motivating ourselves to do it. It becomes an automatic response. If you can keep up your daily training, even for a few minutes a day for thirty days, you will find you have created such a habit. You will no longer have to remind yourself to get up and get on with training, it will have become second nature to you. To maximise your chances of sticking to the programme, get the habit right first and build up the duration of your sessions later.

What Total Recall will not do for you

This programme cannot work miracles. It is important to bear in mind that with animals, you only get what you train for. This Recall Training Programme is not intended to achieve a recall under rare, bizarre or extreme conditions. It will not give you a recall under gunfire for example, either in the military sense or on a recreational shoot. Your dog may recall under such conditions or he may not – but you haven't trained for it and should, therefore, not expect it. Nor will Total Recall guarantee you a recall if your dog is injured or very frightened. Dogs can fall apart under these conditions just as people do. It won't guarantee you a recall in the aftermath of a road traffic accident or if your dog is set upon by other dogs. It is not normally practicable or worthwhile training a domestic dog to cope with these kinds of situations, and you cannot expect Total Recall in conditions which are extraordinary and for which your dog has not been prepared.

It is helpful to know that the more types of recall you train for, the more likely your dog will be to recall in an extraordinary situation, but it is important not to endow this, or any other training programme, with impossible capabilities. Nor should you ever gamble your dog's life on his recall. Total Recall is not a state of mind or a cast-iron guarantee. It is simply a trained response. The more you train, the better it will get. Practice really does make perfect.

What Total Recall will do for you

What Total Recall will get you is an effective and polished recall response in all of the normal situations in which you and your dog are likely to find yourselves – on the beach, in a park, on a moor or in a forest and whether there are other people or animals present. If you call, your dog will come quickly back to you. And by the time you get to the end of the training programme you will have earned the right to be exceptionally proud of your dog, and proud of yourself, too.

You are not alone in the journey you are about to undertake. Whatever mistakes you have made in the past, others have made too. Put them all behind you now. Make sure that each stage in training is thoroughly learned before progressing on to the next. Think of your recall training as a pyramid – the bigger the foundations on which you base your more advanced training, the more stable the whole structure will be. Take it slowly and focus on one stage at a time.

Are you ready to begin? Then let's get started!

PART **2**

Training the Recall

- Puppy Recall

- Pre-recall for Older Dogs

- Basic Recall

- Proofing with People

- Proofing with Dogs

- On Location

- Putting it All Together

- Recall for Life

CHAPTER 9

Puppy Recall

If you are lucky enough to be recall training a small puppy, you have some distinct advantages over those who are training or retraining an older dog. The beauty of training puppies is that they haven't yet learned any bad habits and they come with some wonderful instincts that enable us to establish some initial recall behaviour with little or no effort. I call these instincts the 'safety response' and the 'chase response'. Let's find out how these two useful and inbuilt behaviours will help us.

The safety response

At the first sign of anything scary, a puppy will instinctively head for the nearest 'grown-up' and try to get 'underneath' them. This may seem like an unnecessary tripping hazard, but it made good sense for the pup's ancestors in a world fraught with danger, and where 'grown-ups' were nimble, four-footed and fierce. In addition, the same safety response ensures that the pup will follow his 'grown-ups' to the ends of the earth. This was an essential survival trait in a world where to be left behind meant certain death.

This safety response, which ensures your puppy will follow you whenever he thinks you are leaving him behind or whenever he feels scared, is very useful. It does not last for long, so it is important to take advantage of it when you can, as much as you can. Sadly, many new owners keep their new puppies on a lead until the safety response is all but gone, and so miss out completely on this perfect opportunity to set some excellent foundations for the recall. Fortunately, we have another trick up our sleeves to add to the safety response, and that is the 'chase response'.

The chase response

Many dogs really love to chase a moving object. This is a reminder that the dog is essentially an efficient predator capable of running down his dinner. While we have 'bred out' the chase response in adults of some domestic dog breeds, many young dogs enjoy chasing people to some extent. This passion for chasing helps us to keep puppies running after us, even after the safety response is diminishing.

The puppy recall utilises the safety and chase responses to get puppies into the important habit of racing up to their owners. The whole process is so enjoyable for the puppy that you don't need to use food or any other additional reward at this point. However, giving the puppy an edible treat when he reaches you will make him quite ecstatic about the whole experience, will get him used to being hand-fed outdoors, and will stand you in good stead when the safety response is gone.

Working in combination, these two instinctive behaviours virtually guarantee the small puppy will find chasing after his owner irresistible. This means we can get a puppy to move towards us at any time and that no compulsion, manipulation or force is necessary.

This first exercise, 'Whistles are great', is aimed at building an association between the recall whistle, pleasure and the act of moving towards you. This is where we establish the behaviour we want (i.e. movement towards you), and then pair it with the recall signal. An ideal place to begin is at your puppy's mealtimes. Your puppy will be on four meals a day to begin with, so you will be able to do the following exercise four times a day. After a couple of days you can begin to work on exercise two,

This four-month-old puppy enjoys chasing his young handler

but keep practising exercise one for the next week or so to help build a really strong association between your recall whistle and coming to you for food. Blow the whistle very softly during these exercises. Later on, when the dog is further away, you will be able to use the whistle at 'full power'.

EXERCISE ONE **Whistles are great**

1. Prepare your puppy's meal but don't give it to him yet

2. Attract his attention (rattle his bowl or rustle his food bag) so that he is eager to get at the food

3. Take a step backwards so that your puppy moves towards you, and then blow the whistle softly 'pip-pip-pip-pip-pip' several times in an upbeat and friendly way

4. Let the puppy catch up with you, say 'Good!'* and place his food on the floor as you do so

5. Repeat every mealtime

* The word 'Good!' is your reward marker. Try and say this in a consistent and distinctive way. Make it sound upbeat, snappy and very approving. Some people prefer to use the word 'Yes!'. It does not matter which you choose as long as you always use the same word that the puppy associates with a reward. In the future, this word will help you bridge any time lag between your puppy's obedient response and the moment at which you give him his reward. Use your reward marker every time you give your puppy any kind of edible treat – this will help him to feel good whenever he hears the word.

In the next exercise, you will be encouraging the puppy to move towards you on occasions other than mealtimes. The key to getting this second exercise right is in remembering not to add the recall command until the puppy is on his way towards you as fast as his little legs can carry him. The idea is to build a strong association between your recall signal and the action of racing towards you. Choose an enclosed space where your puppy is safe – your yard or garden are fine, or (later on, vaccinations permitting) a safe field or meadow. There must be no other dogs present.

The best way to put space between you and the puppy in the following exercise is to wait until he has wandered off a little way. When the pup takes his attention away from you and starts investigating a leaf or interesting smell, sneak a few feet away. If the puppy does not take his eyes off you and will not leave you, the place you have chosen for this exercise may be a bit too scary. Try again in a more familiar place where he feels safe enough to leave your side for a short time. If he is very new, you might need to wait a few more days for him to settle in to his new home before trying this again. Here are the steps for the exercise.

EXERCISE TWO Follow my leader

1. Put your puppy down on the ground and watch him as he explores

2. Put a few feet of space between you and the puppy

3. Once the puppy is a few feet away, wait for him to look at you and then run a short distance away from him

4. As soon as the puppy starts moving towards you, crouch down low and give your recall whistle 'pip-pip-pip-pip-pip!', give the signal one time only

5. If the puppy stops moving towards you, move away from him until he starts towards you again

6. As he reaches you, get right down on the ground and let him climb on you and give you a good licking while you feed him one of your basic treats and tell him how fantastic he is

7. Repeat this game many times until your puppy is at least twelve weeks old and has had a minimum of two weeks of regular daily practice

If the puppy is at the older end of the age range, you may need to start this game in an unfamiliar open space in order to trigger the safety response. A 'short distance' means just a few feet to begin with.

The most common mistake people make at this stage is to start calling the puppy before he moves towards them. Please do not be tempted to do this. If you call and he does not come he will have failed. He will also have learned to ignore your whistle. Both are situations that we want to avoid throughout this training process. Remember, don't start calling until he is on his way to you.

What if he doesn't follow me?

If your puppy is under three months old and was a little hesitant about coming right in close to you, something you are inadvertently doing is probably intimidating him. You need to make yourself more desirable to him. It is OK to make some little squeaking noises to attract his attention. If the pup comes in slowly or hesitantly this time, have a premium treat ready for next time.

Keep your voice soft, high and upbeat. This is easier for women, but men can do it too. Be careful not to stare at the pup as some find this very intimidating. Back away from him quickly if he starts to slow down, and have your reward ready to give him the minute he reaches your side. Stick with the premium rewards until you have at least five consecutive rapid, keen approaches. At this point you can give basic rewards some of the time. After a few sessions with basic rewards intermingled with premium ones, you can drop the premium rewards (for the time being).

Beware the tripping hazard

Mind you do not trip over him, or tread on him; new puppies often get right under your feet. Only run a few feet – you are not trying to scare him, or exhaust him, just to trigger his natural instinct to follow you. You are conditioning him to associate the recall whistle with the act of running towards you. Trust that he will make this association. Do not, at any point, use your recall command when the puppy is not already on his way. If you need your pup to come to you for some reason, attract his attention with a handclap, and make off in the opposite direction. He will soon come racing after you and you can reward him.

Involving family members

Children can be very good at this game if they are old enough to avoid stepping on the puppy. Most want to play with a pup and if you teach them to get the puppy to chase after them, instead of the other way around, you are building excellent habits in your dog (and kids). Just tell them that they must take it in turns and that just before the puppy reaches them they must fall to the ground and let the pup jump all over them. Children especially like the part where they let the puppy catch them. If you don't have children, now is your chance for a second childhood. Get that pup running after you, let him think he has caught you, and let him give you a good licking.

This is all about creating a link in your dog's brain, between your recall command and the action of moving towards you. The objective is to ensure your dog loves that recall whistle, and that for now he only ever hears it when he is rushing towards you. We want him to know, without question, that coming to you and being next to you is the best thing in his world.

Remember that this stage is all about building a connection between sound and deed and it is vital that the recall is not used unless the action we want to associate it with is already in progress.

You can also do some work on this conditioning progress in the house. Simply have your whistle and treats to hand, and at a time when you are alone with your puppy crouch down on the floor and attract his attention. If he rushes towards you blow the whistle and reward when he arrives. If he doesn't come to you then keep quiet. You can try again another time. The more you pair the whistle with the recall behaviour the better.

Once your puppy is around twelve weeks old and has had at least a couple of weeks of practising this exercise, you can begin to work on teaching your puppy that the recall whistle actually tells him to do something.

Responding to the signal

Your puppy has had a lot of fun over the last few weeks, chasing after you and listening to your recall word and whistle at the same time. Now you can begin to fade the triggers (running away from the puppy, squeaky noises etc.) that you initially used to encourage the puppy to race after you. In their place you will be gradually establishing your recall whistle as the signal for your puppy to rush towards you.

Keep it simple

There are many ways to make the following exercises harder. Don't be tempted to use them yet. For example, don't attempt these exercises when the puppy is tired or when he is eating. Don't do it when he is sleepy, or when he has noticed something fascinating 'just over there' and so on. Keep it simple. It is easier to begin the 'recall and run' outdoors where you can get up some speed if necessary to initiate the chase response. Practise several times a day, every day. Start by rewarding every single recall. When the puppy responds every time, for several sessions, you can fade the food rewards back to one in every three or four responses. Vary the frequency of rewards a little to keep him guessing. Remember, no distractions and no testing!

EXERCISE THREE **Recall and run!**

For the first time now you are going to use the recall whistle before the puppy starts to move toward you. Use premium rewards to start with and have a sufficient amount so that you can give the puppy a big bonus of several pieces if necessary. To minimise the possibility that the puppy might not respond, you will trigger the chase response immediately after giving the recall command.

1. Put the puppy down in a safe place

2. Put some space between you and the puppy

3. Give the recall signal clearly one time, and one time only, then immediately...

4. Run away from the puppy!

5. Reward the puppy with food when he arrives, crouch down and make a big fuss of him

6. Repeat steps 1 to 5 several times a day, every day for three days

If you are successful after your first three days, start replacing some of the premium rewards with basic rewards. After a few more days you can drop the premium rewards altogether and in their place just give cuddles or praise. With all but the most biddable, 'touch hungry' dogs, you should keep rewarding about half of the recalls with basic rewards.

What if he doesn't chase me this time?

If at any time your puppy does not immediately chase after you as you run away, do NOT on any account repeat your new recall signal. Your job now is to do whatever it takes to get that puppy to start heading towards you, and you need to praise him every step of the way. Crouch down, make noises, clap your hands or run faster. Whatever it takes. And when he reaches you give him a generous bonus reward. Give him chunk after chunk of lovely roast chicken or some other tasty reward. Break it into tiny bits and give them to him one at a time. Make this feeding bonanza last a full minute if you can.

Consider whether or not you made the exercise too difficult (by calling him when he was investigating an interesting smell, for example). Consider also whether you have been sufficiently generous and mindful of rewards over the last few days – fading rewards can interfere with your training.

Remember, too, that there mustn't be any distractions at this stage. This exercise is unlikely to work if, for example, your children are playing on the other side of the fence or if there are other dogs around.

If you are sure that you carried out the exercise correctly, and if the puppy is under three months old, go back to exercise two for another week before trying exercise three again.

Before you begin your second attempt at exercise three, you will need to take steps to make chasing you even more attractive for your puppy. You can do this in two ways: by increasing the distance between you and the puppy when you start to run; or by carrying out the exercise in a more unfamiliar place.

Your puppy is growing in confidence every day, and if he feels completely safe in his own garden, for example, the safety response is less likely to work. Try a friend's garden next time or a larger open space in a field or large park.

Both of these strategies (greater distances and unfamiliar places) increase the dependent puppy's need to be with his protector. Once you are achieving regular success with exercise three, and your puppy is at least three months old, it is time to move on to exercise four.

Recall and walk

Exercise four is the next step in helping your puppy to understand that the recall signal is a cue for him to get moving towards you. Once you have been practising 'recall and run' several times each day for a week or more, and the puppy comes to you every single time (and you have faded the rewards), you can begin to further diminish the power of the movement 'trigger' that you have been using to get him to rush towards you. You will begin to walk, rather than run. A running person is much more attractive than a walking one, but by now the previous exercise will have exerted a training effect and, provided he is not distracted, your puppy will automatically move towards you on hearing the recall signal. Because of the preparation you have done, this will work even though you pose a less attractive sight as you walk calmly away from him.

EXERCISE FOUR **Recall and walk**

As with any change in the level of difficulty of a task, we are going to go back to rewarding every single recall to begin with. Use premium rewards to start with.

1. Put the puppy down in a safe place

2. Put some space between you and the puppy. Try to get at least ten yards away from him for this exercise

3. Give the recall signal and then without hesitation...

4. Walk briskly and calmly away from the puppy. Keep walking as he starts to run after you and turn to face him as he arrives

5. Reward the puppy when he reaches you, making a big fuss of him

6. Repeat steps 1 to 5 several times a day for at least three days

7. Repeat for several more days, gradually reducing the value of the rewards as in the previous exercise

By the end of this exercise you will have a puppy that is thoroughly conditioned to move towards you when he hears the whistle. The sight of you moving away as he comes after you helps keep his enthusiasm high and ensures that he returns to you with joy and passion.

Crouch down low to welcome the puppy in

When is it time to move on?

The next stage in training is the basic recall. Most pups are ready for this stage somewhere between four and five months old. There is no need to be in a hurry to move a puppy on to the basic recall. The whole time he is in the puppy recall stage and flying towards you every time you whistle, his bond with you is strengthening. If your puppy is still a bit clingy or anxious it is better to wait a while. Remember to take advantage of every free opportunity that your puppy provides you with to condition that signal. Every time he runs towards you, blow the whistle. One signal per recall.

If you can answer yes to the following questions, you are ready to move on to the basic recall:

- Have you spent at least two weeks on the Recall and Walk exercise?

- Does your puppy consistently return quickly when you call him?

- Is your puppy at least four months old?

- Is you puppy happy and confident outdoors?

Skip the next chapter, *Pre-recall for Older Dogs*, and go straight to chapter eleven, *Basic Recall*. Much of this will be very easy for your puppy because he has had the advantage of the outdoor exercises in this section. However, it is all good practice for him and with such a young puppy you have no need to hurry. Let's get the foundations well and truly in place before we start to build upwards.

CHAPTER 10

Pre-recall for Older Dogs

This chapter is designed to help prepare the older dog for the exercises in the next chapter. Most older dogs will have learnt bad recall habits to some degree, and we have to counteract those in a very thorough way. Please don't be tempted to skimp on rewards or rush over this early conditioning. It is the foundation of your future recall training and needs to be solidly put in place.

Puppies

This chapter is not for you if your puppy is under five months old. If you have a young puppy, you need to work your way through the previous chapter, *Puppy Recall*, and then move on to the next chapter, *Basic Recall*. If your puppy is at least six months old, this chapter is probably the best place to begin your Recall Training Programme. This is because the puppy recall procedures outlined in the previous chapter do not work as effectively on older puppies. If your pup is borderline in age, is still quite clingy when you are out and about and enjoys chasing you if you run away, then it is definitely worth attempting the Puppy Recall to begin with.

The following exercises all take place indoors, away from distractions. They are all focused around your dog's food and take advantage of the pleasure he gets from eating.

Countering bad habits

Older dogs have often learnt to ignore their owners' shouts and calls, or to come back in their own sweet time. These dogs rarely associate their owner with any kind of powerful reward, and we need to be diligent and patient in re-establishing a solid recall habit.

Most of the bad habits that older dogs have fallen into are formed outdoors. An older dog is well aware of the pleasures to be had by running off to roll in fox poo, playing with other dogs and so on, and we have to be very careful to reintroduce distractions very slowly and in a controlled manner. All of the exercises in this pre-recall section take place well away from distractions of any kind.

If you are retraining a dog that has been running away from you outdoors, please do read chapter nineteen, *The Absconder*, before you begin your training.

A new command

I am going to reiterate here the importance of a new recall command for your dog. Don't be tempted to use an old 'poisoned' command that he associates with a whole range of consequences you probably haven't even thought of. As far as your dog is concerned, if it means anything at all, your old command is more likely to mean 'please yourself' than it is to mean 'rush to my side'. This is not useful. So ditch your old and worthless command and get yourself a nice shiny new one.

Your objectives

The objective of pre-recall training is to condition an association in your dog's mind between the sound of your whistle, the pleasure of a reward and the act of moving towards you or being in close proximity to you. Do not under any circumstances be tempted to use the new whistle to recall your dog yet. We do not want this lovely fresh start to be spoiled by failure, nagging or pleading. All we want initially is for the whistle to be associated with pleasure and your company.

We want these three things...

- You

- Pleasure

- Whistle

...to be inextricably entwined. This takes time and repeated exposure to the associated events. This is not about teaching your dog to 'do' anything, but about forming deep links in his brain. And the more frequently we associate these three things with one another, the sooner this process will be complete.

The wow factor

We are going to make sure that this brand new recall command is inextricably linked with the 'wow factor'. We want your dog to be blown away by your generosity. So put away your boring old biscuits and prepare your premium rewards. You will need lots of nice juicy mouth-wateringly good chunks of delicious meat. You can prepare it in advance but it will smell better to the dog if it is warm or at least at room temperature rather than refrigerated.

The next exercises are very simple ones that you should be able to fit into your day at your convenience.

EXERCISE ONE **Whistle equals wow!**

For this first exercise we are simply going to blow the recall whistle quite softly, every time your dog eats the amazing treats you have put aside for him. Get some of your premium rewards out of the refrigerator and warm them up or leave them out of reach of the dog to come to room temperature.

How often you can carry out this exercise during the day is up to you, but three or four times is ideal.

1. Have the plate of juicy meaty chunks close to hand.

2. Take some of the delicious meat in your closed hand. Don't give it to the dog yet. Have your whistle ready. Do NOT use the whistle to call the dog, you can attract his attention in some other way.

3. Make the dog aware you have some food. If necessary waft it under his nose.

4. Blow the whistle 'pip-pip-pip-pip-pip' gently

5. Open your hand so that the dog can take the meat

6. Then grab another chunk and give those to the dog, and another

7. Feed him several big juicy pieces in a row. You want this to be memorable

That's it for now. You have just made a new noise and given the dog a fantastic treat at the same time. So far, this is just a coincidence; it only took a few seconds. But this is a big moment, a significant moment. It is the very first time that your dog has heard your precious new recall command, and from today, from now on, every time he hears that sound we want him to glow with pleasure.

When you repeat the exercise an hour or two later, your dog's memory will take note that the same new sound happened again with the lovely new treat. Interesting.

Over the next day or two you will repeat this exercise several times. Within a short time your dog will begin to suspect that this amazing tasty treat and this strange new whistle are somehow connected. When you have fed him this way at least ten times over the space of two or three days, it is time to move on to exercise two.

EXERCISE TWO **Whistle means dinner *or* wow**

Now we are going to make the wow rewards a little unpredictable by alternating them with more normal food. You can use your dog's regular food for this. Just divide his normal dinner into portions. If you can fit four sessions in per day then you will need to divide his dinner into two portions. The other two sessions you will use your special delicious meaty chunks. If you can fit six sessions in then divide his dinner into three, and so on.

1. Prepare a portion of your dog's normal food but don't give it to him yet. Have your whistle ready

2. Do not call the dog. Attract his attention by rattling his dish, for example, and when he is next to you...

3. Blow your whistle signal 'pip-pip-pip-pip-pip'

4. Say 'Good!' and place his dinner on the floor

5. Wait at least two hours and then repeat using the fantastic and special meaty treats you gave him yesterday

You can practise this between meals by keeping some mini portions of the dog's food, or some treats, where you can easily reach them and hand feeding them to him at intervals throughout the day. Just make sure you do not blow the whistle unless you are ready to follow up immediately with a meal or some juicy premium rewards.

Keep this up for a few days and aim for your dog to have heard the whistle at least ten times while eating alternately fantastic and regular food. You have now created the beginning of an association in your dog's mind between pleasure (eating) and the whistle, and, incidentally, within close proximity to you. Now we are going to build on that association by adding some movement towards you into the equation.

Opposite ► *Be ready with the whistle*

EXERCISE THREE **Moving dinners**

To initiate some recall activity in your dog that we can link to our command we are simply going to walk backwards with the dog's meal while using the new recall command.

1. Prepare your dog's meal but don't give it to him yet

2. Attract the dog's attention without saying anything (rattle his bowl or rustle his food bag) and stand facing him, making sure that there is a clear space behind you

3. Start to back away from the dog and as he starts to walk towards you give your recall command 'pip-pip-pip-pip-pip' one time only, and then stand still

4. When the dog reaches you, place the food on the floor and say 'Good!' in an upbeat way

5. Repeat every mealtime, every day, for several days. Remember to keep your word 'Good!' upbeat and consistent

If you are at home during the day, divide his daily food ration into three or four smaller ones to enable more practice sessions. Try to get at least ten moving dinner exercises in before moving on to the next chapter. After the first day or two you can alternate these with the moving treats exercise below.

EXERCISE FOUR **Moving treats**

This is just a slightly less-powerful version of exercise three. Try and find as many occasions as you can when you can practise the following steps. Throughout this exercise, remember that the dog should never hear that whistle unless he is moving towards you.

1. Have some treats in your hand or pocket

2. Attract the dog's attention without saying anything (we don't want to build confusing associations with other words). You can throw him a

couple of treats first if you like. Make sure that there is a clear space behind you

3. Start to back away from the dog and as he starts to walk towards you give your recall command 'pip-pip-pip-pip-pip'

4. Stop walking and as the dog reaches you say 'Good!' and feed him a treat.

5. Repeat often and remember to keep your word 'Good!' upbeat and consistent

Blow the whistle as the dog moves towards you

Remember, never to use your new recall command to initiate the recall. You are only using the new recall whistle to 'accompany' the recall behaviour, not to make it happen. This is the conditioning or signal-association component of training.

Now practise this exercise in several different rooms in your home. This helps the dog to begin to associate the whistle with walking towards you in many different places.

Isn't this a bribe?

If you need to throw the dog some treats to attract his attention and get him moving towards you, then you are correct in thinking that this is, in effect, a bribe. You are clearly giving the dog the impression that you are in 'food dispensing mode'. That is OK at this point. When we use a bribe to encourage a dog to move or take up a position, we call it a lure. Using a lure is perfectly acceptable at this conditioning stage, as we are not trying to train your dog to take responsibility for his actions yet. We are simply establishing a link in his mind between the action of moving towards you and the sound of the whistle.

Keep it simple

Don't be tempted to try this when other people are about, or, indeed, outside your home. This new 'association' is fragile and easily destroyed. Keep it simple and practise as often as you can.

DO NOT test your dog and try to use the whistle at any time other than when he is moving towards you and you have food ready to reward him. Do not allow anyone else to do this either. Give the dog a chance to soak up this new information without any potential for failure.

If you can answer 'yes' to the following questions, you are ready to move on to the next stage of training, *Basic Recall*.

• Has your dog heard the recall whistle while he is eating his dinner on at least ten different occasions?

• Has your dog heard the recall whistle while moving towards you for a treat on at least ten different occasions, and in at least three different parts of your house?

- Have you been practising these pre-recall exercises for at least a week?

- Really?

Then it's time to move on!

You do not yet have a recall command. But you do have a new and powerful training tool. You have a sound that your dog firmly associates with moving towards you and with a feeling of great pleasure. Let's move on to *Basic Recall* and begin building that command.

CHAPTER 11

Basic Recall

B y the time you finish the Basic Recall, your dog will thoroughly understand that the recall command actually has an important meaning. It is not just a sound that happens to be associated with you and with food; it is a sound that means 'go to The Boss now'. However, there is an important proviso – your dog will only understand the meaning of this command when it is used in certain, specific circumstances. Namely at home and when there are no distractions.

We need to establish this basic understanding before we begin to add new layers of difficulty. It is important that you spend sufficient time making sure that your dog thoroughly understands the recall command under these limited circumstances, before attempting to proof this skill against the distractions available to him in the big outdoors.

Most dogs will pass through this stage very quickly and usually without problems.

Beginning indoors

If you have moved on from the puppy recall, some of these exercises might seem like a step backwards. After all, you have had your puppy outside, galloping after you with enthusiasm from quite a few yards away already. However, many of this book's early exercises in proofing take place indoors, because this is where we have most control over a wide range of factors, and where we can best set the dog up to win. Only when the dog has achieved success in this controlled environment do we increase the factors of difficulty and move into more challenging locations. If you have moved on from the puppy recall, your dog will still need to practice these 'indoor' exercises.

Our first task, therefore, is to establish a very reliable basic recall, indoors, in very controlled conditions, so that we can build on this solid foundation in structured steps.

Keeping a record

Each exercise needs to be completed a minimum number of times before moving on to the next one, and with the inevitable gaps between them you will soon forget how many times you have done each one.

I suggest you keep a little notebook, or perhaps a list on your fridge, where you make a mark every time you complete another example of a particular exercise.

No distractions, no testing

These sessions should be a very private matter between you and your dog. Unlike with the puppy recall, involving other members of your family in most of these exercises is not recommended. Try to avoid demonstrating your new skills to anyone. In demonstrating how clever your dog is, you are testing him in front of other people, and quite possibly setting him up to fail. We will introduce other people soon enough.

One more important thing to remember is that your recall command has a unique and special purpose. It should be treated with the greatest respect and never used lightly. Hang on to that whistle, it's yours! And don't let anyone else persuade you to 'let them have a go' with it.

Special rewards

Throughout this training programme, every time we 'raise the bar' and ask the dog to do something more difficult, or in a new or more challenging way, we make the initial 'pay-off' for the dog much more valuable. This helps to cement the dog's understanding in more difficult circumstances. This next exercise is no exception, and the main difference between this exercise and the exercises in *Pre-recall for Older Dogs* is that the whistle has become a cue for action. This is the third component of training, 'Obeying the signal', that we talked about in Part One.

When the dog hears the whistle, he now has to figure out that he needs to get next to you. And when he is successful, he needs an impressive reward to confirm that he made the right choice. So it's back to the premium rewards again. Have plenty of them available in case you need to give the dog a bonus reward.

EXERCISE ONE **Same room recall**

Have your treats ready on a raised surface or in your treat bag. Make sure that the dog is in the same room as you, that the two of you are alone, that he is wide awake and that he is not overly preoccupied with another interesting activity (he should not be chewing a toy or eating a meal, for example).

You will need to busy yourself in the room so that the dog relaxes and ignores you. Don't give your dog any additional cues apart from the whistle. No patting your leg or calling his name to begin with. We want to give him a chance to respond to the whistle alone. The conditioning exercises that we carried out in the previous chapter make it quite likely that he will.

1. Put some space between you and the dog (a few steps is fine)

2. Blow the recall whistle softly, just one string of pips 'pip-pip-pip-pip-pip'

3. When the dog reaches you tell him 'Good!' and give him a juicy premium treat

4. Now turn away and wait for him to lose interest so that you can repeat the exercise

5. Repeat at least five times, in the same room, over the course of the day

6. Increase the distance between you and the dog as much as you can but stay in the same room

Because you have already conditioned the dog to associate your new signal with both the delivery of special rewards and the act of moving towards you, the chances are high that he will rush to your side. But what if the dog doesn't come? What if he ignores the signal?

If the dog ignores you do NOT repeat the new recall cue. Take immediate action to make yourself completely irresistible. Crouch down and make squeaky or kissy sounds with your mouth, or anything else that your dog finds appealing. Now you can pat your leg, roll on your back, or do whatever is required.

Use your reward marker 'Good!' to let him know when he is on the right track. Just get the dog to you, and as soon as he reaches you tell him 'Good!' followed immediately by a bonus reward. Several chunks of your mega lovely juicy delicious reward. This will increase the chances of him coming to you next time.

Generous rewards in these early exercises will help ensure that we get a good response established from the beginning. Repeat the exercises with generous rewards until your dog is responding immediately to your recall signal with no extra encouragement from you.

Practising exercise one and reducing rewards

Once your dog can successfully complete five 'same room recalls' in a row, without any encouraging noises or behaviour from you, then repeat the exercise the following day but with normal treats for four recalls and a special juicy treat reserved for just one of the five recalls. If the dog is successful on this basis, then on the following day repeat with normal treats for three recalls and no treat at all for two.

Provided you are not experiencing any recall failures, you are now ready to move on to exercise two. If the dog is failing to come without hesitation, if you are having to offer him extra motivation (squeaking, leg patting etc.) to get him to you, then you need to revert to a continuous schedule of high-value rewards, and fade them out more gradually once you get the behaviour you want.

EXERCISE TWO **New room recall**

For this exercise you will start by choosing a different room and repeat the whole of exercise one in this new room. Before you start, you will need your premium rewards again. You will reward the dog with a tasty and valuable reward for every successful recall in this new room. You are now aiming for three in a row. When you get them, repeat with one premium reward and two basic ones. Then repeat again with two basic rewards and one 'no reward' recall.

1. Put some space between you and the dog (a few steps is fine).

2. Blow the recall whistle softly, just one string of pips 'pip-pip-pip-pip-pip'

3. When the dog reaches you tell him 'Good!' and give him one juicy treat

4. Now turn away and wait for him to lose interest so that you can repeat the exercise

When your dog is consistently coming in to you, in this new room, it's time to practice in one of the other rooms in your home that the dog is allowed access to. Take yourself into yet another new and different room, where we are going to call him in to you.

The same conditions apply; the dog should be awake and relaxed. Don't try to train the dog when you know the kids are about to arrive home from school, or when the dog has just finished a large and satisfying meal.

EXERCISE THREE **Recall from room to room**

Wait until the dog is relaxing in one room and take yourself off into an adjoining room. If he follows you, you'll just have to try again later. Once the two of you are in adjoining rooms (with the door open) you will whistle the dog. Here is how it goes:

1. Wait until the dog is relaxed (but *not* asleep) and leave the room

2. Blow the recall whistle from the adjoining room, just one string of pips 'pip-pip-pip-pip-pip'

3. When the dog reaches you tell him 'Good!' and give him a juicy treat

4. Now wait for him to lose interest so that you can repeat the exercise

Frequently call the dog from one room to another until he comes reliably every time. Use generous rewards to get the behaviour established and reduce them gradually.

Analyse any failures

If your dog fails to recall at any time during this programme you need to ask yourself, before you try the exercise again:

• Was something distracting the dog?

If you are confident that the dog was not being subjected to an unplanned distraction (a car door banging in the road outside or a child's voice in the garden next door, for example) then the next question is:

• Did I make the task too difficult?

Did you call the dog from too far away or did you call from a new place in the house without reducing the distance, for example. If you have moved on too quickly you will need to back up to an easier exercise for a while.

If you are confident that neither of these apply, make sure that you have plenty of impressive rewards available before the next attempt and ensure that the dog is really hungry.

However, in most cases you will not need this advice. At this stage, the dog will be only too keen to get himself next to you as soon as he hears the magical sound that has come to be associated with a wonderful treat.

Whatever happens, try to remember that dogs are simple souls and that if he is not doing as you wish, it isn't personal. He just hasn't figured it out yet. Your responsibility is to make the exercise easier, break it down into smaller chunks, or practice more frequently until he gets it. Don't be tempted to think that he doesn't deserve a great reward because he didn't make the effort to rush to you immediately. It is vital that you develop the skill of switching into friendly and generous mode whenever your dog reaches your side, no matter how annoying he was being thirty seconds ago. Greeting him through gritted teeth will not help your progress at all.

EXERCISE FOUR Recall from sleep

Once you have nailed exercise three, you can try calling the dog when he is fast asleep. Obviously you don't want to deprive him of too much beauty sleep, but it is OK to do this quite a few times. Dogs use sleeping as a way of passing the time until the next walk or meal. He won't become irritable or depressed because you disturb his sleep occasionally.

The principle is exactly the same as before. Start with high-value rewards.

- Put space between you and the dog

- Call the dog

- Reward every success

- Practise with fewer rewards

Learning to recall away from something attractive

Calling a dog away from something he really wants is an important lesson for him. He already understands that your recall command means 'come here' and that the response will often get him what he wants, i.e. a valuable reward. But what if the 'thing' he wants, that same valuable reward, can clearly be seen, and it isn't where you are?

Teaching the dog to come away from something very attractive in order to go to you may take a little more patience than the exercises so far. Let's see how it goes!

EXERCISE FIVE Recall from food

In this exercise we will put some of those extra special tasty chunks of meat that we have been using in the initial stages of each exercise on a plate in clear view of the dog, but out of his reach. You will then position yourself so that the dog is between you and the food and call him away from the plate towards you.

Let him see you putting the meat out on the plate. Make sure he is watching you and keen to get at the food.

1. Walk a few steps away from the dog so that he is between you and the food

2. Blow the recall whistle softly 'pip-pip-pip-pip-pip'. Do not repeat the command!

3. If the dog comes straight to you tell him 'Good!' and return to the plate with him to give him a treat

Note the word 'If'. This is difficult for the dog and he may need some more encouragement.

If he does not come

If the dog cannot tear himself away from the plate of tasty treats, do not repeat the cue but make sure the dog comes to you just as you did in exercise one. Encourage the dog to you, praising him each time he glances or makes a move in your direction. Use your reward marker 'Good!' to let him know when he is on the right track. Be patient. Do not worry about how long this takes. He cannot get at the meat and eventually he will give

Coming away from food is hard to do!

up trying and come to you. Tell him 'Good!' and take him straight over to the plate for his reward. Feed him several chunks of the tasty meat from the plate that he was so keenly watching. Then try again.

1. Walk a few steps away from the dog

2. Blow the recall whistle softly 'pip-pip-pip-pip-pip' Do not repeat the command!

3. If the dog comes straight to you tell him 'Good!' and give him a treat

He will come quicker this time. Practise until the dog comes straight to you each time you give a single recall whistle. Never repeat the whistle. Eventually the penny will drop. The dog will realise that going to YOU is the best way to get the thing he wants. When you reach this point the dog will recall over and over again away from the food that he really desires. Eureka!

Making the rewards more exciting

Now you can start to reduce the reward frequency just as you did in the previous exercises, making the reward more exciting to the dog. Sometimes when he recalls away from the food you will NOT take him over for a reward. And sometimes you will.

Now practise all of these recall exercises around your house using a random schedule of rewards. Don't forget that reducing reward frequency in a random manner increases the reliability of your training through the gambling effect. For a day or two, concentrate on making your rewards even more sporadic and unpredictable. Sometimes reward three recalls in a row. Sometimes ask for three recalls in a row without a reward. Sometimes when you whistle, have a real jackpot treat ready for him, a big hunk of chicken or a slice of bacon. Sometimes when you whistle just give him a stroke or a pat as a reward. He will be disappointed, but as long as you don't do it too often it will make him even keener to come the next time.

Gradually reduce the proportion of recalls that you reward to just one in every three or four.

In his own time

Some dogs are naturally effervescent, doing everything at breakneck speed. If this is how your dog behaves during recall, you can skip this following exercise and go straight to the questions at the end. Later on, your only problem will be stopping the dog from bowling you over when he arrives, so enthusiastic is his return! And we look at dealing with that little problem in the final chapter of this book.

Some dogs, however, seem to walk around in a daze. Everything is a bit of a bore, and trying to get an enthusiastic recall from a dog like this is a bit like trying to persuade a teenager that Sundays begin before 2pm.

Basically he just dawdles everywhere, and watching him recall is rather like watching paint dry. If this is your dog then you can help to speed him up by rewarding his recalls more selectively – pick out the faster ones for your rewards and let the slower ones go unrewarded.

This takes a little practice on your part, so don't worry if you don't succeed straight away. You will get better at judging which recalls are the faster ones.

Each day that you practise this exercise your dog will get quicker, up to a point. You are not going to turn a Honda into a Ferrari but you should see some marked improvement within a few days.

Outdoor recall

When you have had plenty of practise with recalling your dog around your house, it is time to show him that the recall signal works outside, too. If your garden or yard is very large, or not adequately fenced, and if you are working with an older dog that has previously proven difficult to catch or bring in from the garden, you must put the dog on a training lead for these exercises. Read chapter twenty-two, *Using a Training Lead*, before you begin.

EXERCISE SIX **One man garden recall**

Take your dog and some premium treats into the garden. Don't forget to wear your whistle. Let the dog relax and sniff about for a bit and wait until he is not focused on anything in particular.

1. Put some space between you and the dog (a few steps is fine)

2. Blow the recall whistle, just one string of pips 'pip-pip-pip-pip-pip'

3. When the dog reaches you tell him 'Good!' and give him a juicy treat

4. Now turn away and wait for him to lose interest so that you can repeat the exercise

5. Repeat several times (twice a day is good) over the course of the next few days

6. Increase the distance between you and the dog to no more than twenty yards

If the dog does not come to you immediately when he hears your whistle, you know what to do. Run, clap, squeak etc. but do not use the whistle again. Practise this exercise until the dog comes immediately to your whistle in the garden without any extra encouragement from you. No squeaking, no running away, no extra help at all. Continue to practise as you reduce the frequency and quality of the rewards.

Congratulations!

Completing this section means you now have a very basic recall – a foundation on which to build. You are ready to begin proofing your new recall command so that it works in a variety of different situations and locations. This will provide you with an excellent recall response that will not crumble when you are out in public with your dog. Right now, your recall is only programmed to work at home.

However, you need to be able to answer yes to each of these questions before moving on:

- Can you call your dog from any room in the house to any other room in the house?

- Can you call your dog away from food?

- Can you recall your dog when you are out in the garden together?

- Does he come quickly every time you call?

- Have you faded the rewards down to about ¼ of all recalls?

We have gone into quite a lot of detail in the exercises and asked you to complete quite a few repetitions of each, especially at the beginning. This is because the more effort you put into getting a perfect response in these earlier exercises, the more smoothly your future training will progress. Now, let's work carefully through the next important stage in training – *Proofing with People*.

CHAPTER 12

Proofing with People

If you have ever stood in a public place trying, unsuccessfully, to call your dog away from a stranger that he is pestering enthusiastically, you will understand how frustrating this can be. For many owners of friendly dogs, recalling their dog away from other people is something they never fully achieve.

There are several exercises in this section, each slightly more challenging for the dog than the last. As soon as the dog is consistently successful at one exercise, you can move on to the next. Recalling your dog away from total strangers in public places is your ultimate objective. But before we move on to this skill in *Putting it All Together*, we are going to lay the foundations for success by practicing using your friends and family, at home, where we can control the training exercise and ensure that the dog experiences success.

For some less people-orientated dogs, recalling away from people is a fairly simple matter, and if your dog is not particularly interested in other people you will probably fly through this section. You should still work through each exercise, however, and take care to ensure that you can answer yes to the questions at the end before moving on.

Very friendly dogs may find this stage quite tough, and in a few cases it may be necessary to spend weeks, rather than days, working on it. To begin with we will minimise the power of the distraction you are introducing as much as we possibly can.

In order to teach your dog to recall away from other people you will need to enlist some help.

Choosing your assistants

You will need a friend to assist with your first exercise. Don't be tempted to use small children, they will probably get the giggles and are unlikely to follow your instructions properly. You will just end up feeling cross with them, and the dog.

At times, your assistant will be asked to keep very still and not speak – speaking increases his attractiveness to the dog and we want to keep this at a minimum to begin with. In later exercises you will need to practise with other assistants, and eventually with people that have not been fully briefed on how to behave. But to begin with we will make it very easy for the dog to succeed, and this means ensuring that he receives no reward for ignoring the recall.

Remember that this is just an introduction to the concept of recalling away from people and that all of these exercises take place at home, where you have more control. You have not taught your dog to recall away from strangers in a park, and as always, your new recall command must not be used in any situation that we have not prepared for.

EXERCISE ONE **Come away from a boring person**

We will begin by making the task as simple as possible. To prepare for this exercise, have some premium treats ready and shut yourself in a room with the dog. Your chosen assistant should be briefed to enter the room on your signal (you can simply say 'Please enter') and to shut the door behind him. He should then stand completely still with his arms folded. He should not speak at all.

1. Shut yourself in the room with the dog

2. Give your signal for your assistant to enter. He will remain standing still at the far end of the room

3. Put some space between you and the dog (a few steps is fine)

4. Blow the recall whistle softly, just one string of pips 'pip-pip-pip-pip-pip'

5. When the dog reaches you, take hold of his collar, tell him 'Good!' and give him a premium treat. Now release him with 'Go play' and when he reaches your assistant, tell your assistant to pet him for a moment or two

6. Now ask your assistant to leave the room and repeat the exercise again from the beginning

When you repeat the exercise, alternate basic and premium rewards a few times and if all continues to go well, stick with basic rewards.

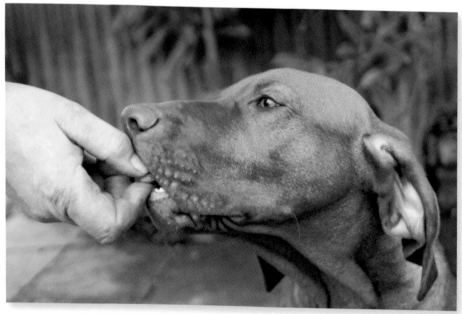

Practise with basic rewards once success is achieved

But what if the dog does not come?

If the dog does not come as soon as you have given the recall signal, the drill is the same as it was in *Basic Recall*. Do NOT repeat the new recall cue. You need to make yourself completely irresistible so crouch down and make squeaky noises or kissy sounds, pat your leg or roll on your back... anything that your dog finds appealing. Ensure that your assistant does not move or make a sound. Get the dog to you and as soon as he reaches you tell him 'Good!' followed immediately by a bonus reward. Think quantity and quality (several chunks of nice juicy meat) and break them up to feed him slowly, making it last.

Now release the dog and let him return to your assistant, who may now pet the dog enthusiastically for a few moments. For very friendly dogs, this attention is what he really wanted and it is an important part of his reward. You can then ask your assistant to leave the room and repeat the exercise.

Weaning off high-value rewards

If you had to use bonus rewards to get this recall going, reduce the frequency of these higher value rewards carefully. Replace the bonus with single premium rewards initially, rather than dropping straight back to basic reward.

Remember, when the dog does not come immediately and needs extra encouragement from you, always give him a higher value reward when he gets it right. You might think he does not deserve it, but that is not the point. We are using the power of consequences to change his behaviour, not making judgements on how deserving he is. If you are mean, why should he bother next time? We can shape a faster recall later, but let's get one established first.

Do NOT be tempted to repeat your recall command. Repeat the exercise with the higher value rewards until he comes immediately to your call, three times in a row. Then gradually reduce the frequency of the higher value rewards, replacing some of them with lower value rewards.

Remember to ensure that the dog gets absolutely no response from your assistant until he has completed the recall.

You can move on to exercise two when your dog has completed exercise one successfully, three times in a row, with just the basic reward. When we move on to exercise two we use higher value rewards again to begin with.

Exercise two is a little harder for the dog because we encourage your assistant to pet the dog before attempting to recall him. It is, however, very hard indeed for a friendly dog to 'break away' while a person continues to pet him, so ask your assistant to stop petting and become 'boring' again as soon as we give the recall signal.

EXERCISE TWO **Come away from a friendly person**

Set this exercise up exactly the same way as exercise one, but brief your assistant as follows. In this exercise your assistant will greet the dog calmly when he enters the room and stroke him quietly, but as soon as you recall the dog your assistant will straighten up, fold his arms and ignore the dog as before. He then gets no more attention until he completes the recall

1. Shut yourself in the room with the dog. Have some premium treats to hand

2. Give your signal for your assistant to enter. He can stroke the dog and greet him quietly but should not get the dog overexcited!

3. Put some space between you and the dog (a few steps is fine)

4. Blow the recall whistle softly, just one string of pips 'pip-pip-pip-pip-pip'

5. When the dog reaches you take hold of his collar, tell him 'Good!' and give him a premium treat. Now release him with 'Go play' and when he reaches your assistant, tell your assistant to pet him for a moment or two.* This time he can be more enthusiastic

6. Now ask your assistant to leave the room and repeat

*Note: The attention paid to the dog by your assistant after each successful recall is part of the dog's reward. For a very friendly dog it is probably the most important part, so don't leave it out.

Once the dog is successful at recalling during a calm greeting, you can start recalling him while your assistant is making much more of a fuss of him.

The next exercise will help to further confirm to your dog that the best route to all good things lies through you.

EXERCISE THREE Come away from a person with food

Now we are going to make your assistant seriously attractive to food-orientated dogs. Give your helper some really tasty premium treats to hold in his hand. Your assistant must not allow the dog to get the treats but must make sure that the dog can smell them and wants to get at them. Your assistant can keep the treat inside a closed fist and should be willing to let the dog lick at his hand. Once the dog has recalled successfully, your assistant must cross the room and feed the dog.

1. Shut yourself in the room with the dog. You will not need any treats

2. Give your signal for your assistant to enter. He must make it clear that he has some nice treats in his hand but make sure the dog cannot get them

3. Put some space between you and the dog (a few steps is fine)

4. Blow the recall whistle softly, just one string of pips 'pip-pip-pip-pip-pip'

5. When the dog reaches you take hold of his collar, tell him 'Good!' This is your assistant's signal to join you and give your dog the treat from his hand

It is highly likely that your dog will not come straight away when you call him. You will need to be patient and encourage him to come to you without repeating the recall. This may take a while but he cannot get what he wants from your assistant and he will eventually look to you for help.

It may take several repetitions of this exercise before the dog reliably recalls away from your food-holding assistant time and time again. Keep practising until you get to this point. Make sure that the dog can respond immediately to your whistle at least half a dozen times in a row, with no extra encouragement from you, before moving on. This is an important milestone. Don't expect too much too soon.

EXERCISE FOUR Come away from a different assistant

This exercise is simply a question of completing all of the exercises in this chapter, but with different people. Remember how poor dogs are at generalising, we don't want him to think that recalling away from a person only applies to your sister-in-law or next door neighbour. So do carry out the exercises with at least one other assistant before moving on to visitors at the door.

Visitors to your home

Calling the dog away from random visitors to your house is good practice for him, but you will need to be a little selective. It is not going to help him if the visitor in question will not stop petting the dog when you ask them to. In this situation it is better to leave recall practice for another time.

The key to success is to brief people in advance that they can fuss over the dog after a successful recall but not before. In each case you will let the person greet the dog briefly, ask them to stop petting the dog for a moment, and then recall him away from them, rewarding him when he arrives. He can then be allowed to return for some more attention. You can also set up 'fake' visits to the house using friends and family, to make sure your dog gets plenty of practice. You will need to keep a supply of treats in the fridge and remember to grab a few when you answer the door.

Into the garden

Recalling in the garden is good practice and helps to prepare the dog for recalling in more open spaces. If you can persuade friends or visitors to help you with the next exercise, it will stand you in good stead. Ideally you will take your dog into the garden and ask your visitor to surprise him by entering unexpectedly. All you have to do is get the dog to come to you. Your visitor has to stop fussing over the dog as soon as you give the recall signal, and ignore him completely until you give the 'Go play' release command.

EXERCISE FIVE Come away from a visitor in the garden

1. Go into the garden with your dog. Have some premium treats to hand

2. Wait for your visitor to enter. He can stroke the dog and greet him quietly but should not get the dog overexcited!

3. Put some space between you and the dog (a few steps is fine)

4. Blow the recall whistle softly, just one string of pips 'pip-pip-pip-pip-pip'

5. When the dog reaches you, take hold of his collar, tell him 'Good!' and give him a premium treat. Now release him with 'Go play' and when he reaches your assistant, tell your assistant to pet him again for a moment or two. This time he can be more enthusiastic

6. Ask your visitor to pretend to leave so that you can repeat the exercise

If the dog does not come when you call, you know what to do. Practise this whenever you get the chance with an obliging visitor. When the dog has the hang of it, you can start replacing the high-value rewards with basic ones.

Don't punish the recall!

Beware of shutting the dog away immediately after a successful recall. A lot of people do this when visitors arrive. Shutting your dog in another room after calling him away from a visitor will have a punishing effect. If you need to shut the dog in another room, do so before you let the visitor in, or after a gap of a few minutes when he has 'said hello'.

When you do remove him from the room, simply lead him calmly away by a lead or his collar without speaking, rather than using your recall word. It really is very important that this special signal is never associated with punishment, and to most dogs, being shut out of the room is a punishment.

Unpredictable rewards

After a few days, and at least ten consecutively successful recalls from a variety of visitors, you can begin to reduce the frequency of rewards. Start to reward every other recall, then every third and fourth. Once in every ten or so recalls give a jackpot (a splendid and extra-special reward). This erratic and unpredictable schedule of rewards helps to fix the new behaviour. This is powerful science in action; don't be afraid to use it.

I didn't have my whistle handy

It is easy to be taken by surprise when you are practising these exercises. If visitors arrive and you don't have your whistle or any treats to hand, then don't recall the dog. Just go and get him. Leave the practising for another day.

The next exercise is a fun one that you can do with a willing helper. It is not essential to do this exercise but it is a nice way to involve a friend or family member at this point. Pick someone that will follow your instructions and not break the rules – especially the rule about more than one command. Make sure your assistant can blow the recall signal in the same way that you do.

EXERCISE SIX **Two man garden recall**

You will need two of everything, apart from the dog! Two whistles and two bags of treats (one each). Take yourselves into your garden. Have your helper hold the dog and stand about ten paces apart. Instruct your helper to hold on to the dog, and to keep holding him for a count of three after you have blown the recall whistle.

1. Walk away from your assistant and your dog

2. Blow the recall whistle softly, just one string of pips 'pip-pip-pip-pip-pip'

3. Your assistant must let him go after three seconds

4. Mark and reward his arrival with a premium treat. Make a big fuss of him

When your assistant lets the dog go, if the dog fails to charge straight towards you immediately, take action. Start moving away from the dog and get the dog coming towards you. Encourage him all the way in then reward generously.

5. If all goes well switch places with your assistant. You hold the dog while he blows the recall. If the dog is unsure about going to your assistant, go with him and let your assistant reward him generously when you get there

Once the dog has grasped the idea and is running confidently back and forth between the two of you, you can begin to stretch out the distance between you. Do this gradually, little by little, as far as the constraints of your garden will allow. Once you have reached the limits of your garden, you can begin to reduce the frequency of higher value rewards. Arm yourselves with some basic treats and begin to switch to these.

This exercise is a great way to give a fit and healthy dog some off-lead running without him getting into mischief. It is also ideal for dogs that are quite clingy as it builds their confidence in running longer distances towards you. Holding onto the dog for a few seconds just builds the excitement a little and gets you a faster, keener recall.

A reminder about repeated commands

At this point in training, a lot of people forget themselves and begin repeating commands. If the dog hesitates, or ignores your command, it is tempting for you to try one more whistle to get him to return. But remember that two commands yesterday becomes three tomorrow, and before you know it you will be back to pleading, begging and shouting. And all your hard work will be lost.

Stick to a single recall command 'pip-pip-pip-pip-pip', and don't be tempted to repeat it.

You are making good progress

You and your dog are doing really well to have reached this point. Completing these exercises at home has formed excellent foundations for the more advanced recall work that you will be doing in the 'real world'. It isn't always easy to set up training exercises in this way, and the willingness and commitment to do so is often what separates the owner of a successfully trained dog from the owner of a disobedient one. It is quite a journey that you have embarked on, and you should be really proud of yourself for getting to this point.

Gradually, bit by little bit, your dog is beginning to embrace the widening scope of the new recall command. Remember to avoid testing your dog in situations that you cannot control or have not prepared for. Find as many opportunities as you can to set him up to win.

Ready to move on?

Before you move on make sure you can answer yes to the questions below:

- Can you reliably recall your dog away from assistants that have been petting him?
- Can you reliably recall your dog away from assistants that have food?

- Can you reliably recall your dog away from visitors at your front door?

- Have you weaned your dog off premium rewards in each of these scenarios?

If so, then it is time to move on to the next chapter where you will be making a start on the challenging concept of recalling your dog away from other dogs.

CHAPTER 13

Proofing with Dogs

Parting company with a potential playmate is a lot more difficult for some dogs than others. If your dog is 'dog friendly' you will take longer to work through this stage in training than someone whose dog does not like other dogs, or is not very interested in them. You may already be familiar with that sinking feeling when your dog has spotted another dog in the distance and you just get his lead on in time... well it's time to change that. You will create a new association between the recall whistle and the act of racing towards you, even in the presence of other dogs.

Just like proofing with people we will train the basic concepts at home, where your dog has already had lots of success and where you can control the outcome of his behaviour relatively easily. In this chapter we will also look at the importance of your dog's attitude towards you and at how we can improve this.

The basic concept

There is a very important concept that we have been introducing to your dog in the previous training chapters. It is the concept of moving away from something he really wants to have in order to be given access to it. This is a very alien concept to a dog; normally a dog gains access to something by moving towards it.

We have already shown the dog that moving away from food, or from a person with food, and towards you when he hears the recall signal is the best way to get access to those things. Those previous lessons have laid good foundations for this one.

How this chapter works

This chapter introduces the concept of recalling away from another dog under very controlled conditions. It will not teach your dog to recall away from a strange dog on the beach or in a park; that comes later in the chapter entitled *Putting it All Together*.

As you start calling your dog away from other dogs, reward every single success to being with. Remember to start with premium rewards and to be ready with some especially generous bonus rewards to help get your new behaviour established. Rewards will be reduced once the dog has grasped the idea.

Even if you are successful very quickly, do not be tempted to try out your commands in new locations just yet. It is vital that the dog is flawless in his response to the recall in your garden before attempting to take this new skill into a more distracting and challenging environment.

Please do remember not to test your dog, but to stick with the programme stage by stage. You are doing really well, it is important not to jeopardise your hard work by rushing the dog on before he is ready.

Your canine assistant

To begin this exercise you will need an assistant with a dog. Your assistant's dog does not need to be highly trained, but it is really important that the dog in question is a fairly calm and friendly animal. Your dog is not going to find it easy to learn to recall away from another dog if the other dog is spinning about on the end of a lead or yapping hysterically. Silly behaviour is likely to be attractive and fascinating to a dog-friendly dog. Nor will it help your dog-friendly dog much if your assistant's dog is unfriendly and wants nothing to do with him. This is because part of the reward for your dog will be the opportunities for play and interaction.

Your ideal helper will be a friend with a sociable dog that is capable of sitting still on a lead while another dog walks past. By the way, it is no good just borrowing someone's dog and trying to set everything up on your own... you will need the help of the owner too!

What if I can't find a friend with a dog to help me?

The only effective way to teach your dog to recall away from other dogs is to train using real dogs. If you cannot be sure that your dog will come away from another dog in your back garden, you have no chance of achieving this anywhere else, therefore you have to find a way of engineering this set-up or something similar. Unfortunately, there is no way around practising a recall in this manner and you cannot skip this training. You are going to meet other dogs when you are out and about. It is inevitable. If you are not able to practise this skill, and your dog is friendly, you are likely to get into difficulties when you meet other dogs outdoors.

If necessary, you may need to pay a local dog trainer for their time to help you with this stage in training. Check beforehand that the trainer is willing to work with food and understands the principles of training with rewards. All trainers who are members of the Association of Pet Dog Trainers should be happy to help you train your dog using effective rewards such as food or toys.

Indoors or out?

In principle, the first exercise in this chapter could initially be carried out indoors. You might find this helpful if the weather is bad. If you need some help from a training lead you can use a shorter version (known as a

If you cannot find a friend to help, you may need to pay a professional trainer

houseline) indoors. In practice, using a training lead around furniture can cause problems with a lively dog and you may not want two dogs bouncing around in your home. It all depends on your circumstances but an indoor session can work in a large room or a long corridor. However, most of you will want to do this in your garden.

Just like in proofing with people, the opportunity to engage with the other dog is a part of your dog's reward. This is especially important if your dog really loves other dogs. You will be giving him a reward of one minute's playtime for obeying your recall. If your dog is not particularly interested in other dogs, then the food part of his reward will be his priority.

EXERCISE ONE **Come away from a dog on a lead**

Have your dogs on leads, take both dogs out into your garden and stand ten paces apart with each dog next to his owner. Your assistant's dog stays on a lead until you give the 'Go play' command. Make sure that your assistant understands he must release his dog the instant he hears you say 'Go play' to your dog. Prompt him if necessary!

1. Stand ten yards away from your assistant

2. Release your dog

3. Let your dog briefly approach the other dog

4. Give the recall command, one time only

5. Encourage the dog in to you, hold him, reward him and tell him 'Go play' as you release him

6. Let the dogs play one minute then collect up the dogs and restart from step 1

If your dog finds this very difficult, have him wear a training lead. Step on the lead only in order to prevent him reaching and poking the other dog. Keep encouraging him back to you. Only when he returns should he receive his reward of a treat and one minute's playtime.

You will also need to have the dog on a training lead if you have problems catching him at the end of the exercise. Do not use your precious new recall for this purpose.

7. Repeat the exercise until your dog recalls away from the other dog as soon as you give your whistle signal, and without any extra encouragement from you

8. Reward him generously every time, until you have at least five successful fast recalls in a row

9. Gradually reduce the frequency and value of your rewards, as before

This takes as long as it takes; it all depends on your dog. Once you have cracked it, you are really making progress. Your dog is now suspecting that the real key to having fun is not to run off and ignore you, that in fact you are the provider of fun and it is a much better idea to stay close by.

Recalling away from another dog can be practised indoors too

Helping each other

If you are working through this programme with a friend, you can take it in turns to be the assistant in these exercises. It can be much easier to work through a training programme with another dog owner, supporting and encouraging each other through the tricky bits.

For the next exercise you will ask your assistant to move about with his dog. All he needs to do is keep walking his dog up and down on the lead. He should ignore your dog completely.

EXERCISE TWO Come away from a moving dog

Start this exercise with both dogs outside on their leads. Brief your assistant to keep moving up and down unless you ask him to stand still.

1. Ask your assistant to walk their dog up and down an imaginary ten-yard path

2. Stand a good five yards to one side of this 'path' and let your dog observe for a moment

3. Now let your dog off the lead and allow him to approach the other dog

4. Before your dog reaches the other dog, recall him

5. Reward your dog with a treat and then release both dogs for one minute's playtime

6. Repeat several times in succession

7. Prevent self-rewarding with your training lead

8. Practise many times until your dog comes rapidly away from the moving dog without hesitation

If your dog does not come back as soon as you have given the recall signal, ask your assistant to stand still while you encourage your dog back to you. Reward generously when the dog arrives.

What does your dog value most?

You will, by now, have an idea of what your dog values the most – his playtime or his treats. If he is keen to eat the premium treats you offer him then make the most of it. Make the first treat in each exercise a real

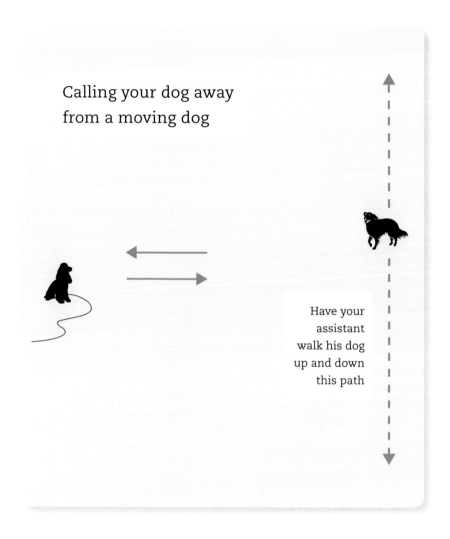

Calling your dog away
from a moving dog

Have your
assistant
walk his dog
up and down
this path

bonus session. Spend as long as twenty seconds feeding him tiny piece
after tiny piece.

If, on the other hand, the best reward is playtime (if he barely glances
at the treat or gulps it down with little interest and just wants to play),
then focus on playtime as the reward. Mark each successful recall clearly
with 'Good!' and release him immediately with 'Go play' so that he knows
without a doubt that his playtime is a consequence of his successful recall.

Spend plenty of time on this exercise and don't attempt the next one
until he is successful at least five times in a row. Do not allow your dog to

reward himself by bouncing around your garden and leaping all over the other dog after you have given the recall signal. If necessary use a training lead to prevent this (see chapter twenty-two).

In this next exercise we will make the assistant dog much more interesting. We will also put the assistant dog on a training lead so that your assistant can prevent him from interfering in your recall.

EXERCISE THREE **Come away from a loose dog**

Start this exercise with both dogs outside on their regular leads. The assistant dog should be wearing a training lead in addition to his regular lead. If your dog needed a training lead for the previous exercise, he should wear one for this exercise too.

Have plenty of rewards ready. Brief your assistant to step on his dog's training lead when you blow the recall. This just prevents the assistant dog from following yours back to you and distracting him from his recall. Make sure you are further from your assistant than the length of the training lead when you recall the dog. Shorten the lead if necessary to achieve this.

1. Release both dogs

2. Allow the dogs to greet each other and play briefly

3. Recall your dog (your assistant should restrain his)

4. Mark the successful recall, feed and release to 'Go play' (your assistant should release his dog at this point) for one minute

5. Repeat

Brevity is important here, don't wait until the dogs are involved in a full-blown game of chase before giving the first recall. The more focused your dog is on playing with the other dog, the more challenging the recall. If you miss your chance, wait for a lull in the action before attempting to recall your dog.

Preparing for the future

Achieving Total Recall is not just about recall training, it is also about managing your dog and the way he spends his free time. In chapter six, *Beyond Training*, we looked at the role managing your dog's off-lead exercise plays in shaping his future behaviour, and in changing his attitude towards you. Now is quite a good time to review that chapter because you are very close to the part where we take the dog out into the real world and begin applying the training you have learned at home in more challenging locations.

One aspect of managing your dog that we need to consider at this point is the way in which you handle your dog's encounters with other dogs.

Your dog's social life

The highly sociable dog often sees other dogs as playmates, toys or objects to be used as a source of entertainment. At the same time, he often sees his owner as a bit of a bore. These two attitudes are interlinked.

Perhaps surprisingly, teaching your dog to recall away from other dogs and, to a certain extent, reducing his opportunities for interaction with other dogs on a free-for-all basis will not make him more desperate to play with other dogs. On the contrary, pestering other dogs is often largely a matter of habit and this training will help to teach your dog a more mature and polite approach to meeting dogs on his trips outdoors, which is actually just good manners.

Many dog owners worry about preventing their dog from interacting with, or approaching, other dogs. They feel that it is important for their dog to have the opportunity to meet and greet any dog he comes across. Some young dogs that have been highly socialised to other dogs are extremely boisterous and playful with every dog they meet. While most dogs tolerate this kind of behaviour quite readily in puppies, it becomes less appealing and more annoying as the bouncy and playful dog grows up. If your dog is like this, you probably find yourself saying 'He only wants to play' in an apologetic voice and on a regular basis to other irate dog owners, while trying to disentangle your dog from one that clearly does not wish to play at all. You may be worried about spoiling your dog's enthusiasm for life and ruining his fun if you try and curtail this behaviour.

While it is important for dogs to be able to play, especially while they are still juveniles, it is perfectly reasonable for this social time to be on your terms and not theirs. It is fine for you to restrict playtime to specific occasions and with specific dogs if you wish. And it is also fine to reduce the amount of overall playtime available to your dog as he matures. It is worth emphasising that in many cases an approach by your dog may not be welcomed by the dog on the receiving end, or by his owner.

Most adult dogs over two years of age don't particularly enjoy playing with strange dogs. Many polite dogs will respond tolerantly to another dog's overtures of friendliness, but would rather be greeted briefly or left alone. They certainly do not appreciate being mugged by your nine-month-old dynamo while taking the air on a previously peaceful Sunday morning.

Your dog's attentions may not always be welcome!

Finally, it is worth bearing in mind that working dogs, such as guide dogs and gundogs, are taught to completely ignore other dogs unless specifically given permission to go and have some free play. If every working dog were allowed to stop and greet every dog he passed during the course of the day, he would never get any work done. Yet working dogs do not suffer from stress-related conditions, anxiety, depression or behavioural problems as a result of this restriction. On the contrary, they are probably among the most well-balanced dogs you will ever meet.

So, while you are working your way through this section of the training programme, and at any time in the future, do not feel badly about restricting your dog's interactions with other dogs in public places. Together with recall training, the end result will be a well-mannered dog that is not a nuisance to others.

Homework!

For some dogs, this skill of moving away from another dog in order to gain an opportunity to play is one of the most difficult things they will ever learn. Very friendly dogs will need a lot of practice before they become fluent in recalling away from another dog in this manner. The more you can practise before we take this whole show on the road, the better.

Try to work through these exercises with a different assistant dog. And if you have been using a training lead, wean the dog off the lead and practise the whole sequence without one. Read chapter twenty-two, *Using a Training Lead*, to find out how to do this.

When you have a perfect response every time, start to reduce the rewards. Sometimes recall the dog and release him, then recall him again immediately without a chance for playtime. Introduce these unrewarded recalls intermittently and occasionally.

It will be really beneficial if you can work through each of these exercises with a different assistant. If you only have one suitable assistant then you might want to consider joining a training class to get some more practice at this important skill.

If you can answer yes to the following questions, it is time to move on to the next stage:

- Can you recall your dog away from another dog in your garden while they are both playing or interacting gently together?

- Can you do the above without your dog wearing a training lead?

- Have you reduced the frequency and value of the rewards that you are offering your dog?

CHAPTER 14

On Location

S o far we have undertaken some proofing of your dog's new recall in a very controlled environment. You have taught your dog a simple recall to whistle, and to recall away from people and other dogs at home and in your garden.

Understandably you are probably not too bothered about whether or not your dog will recall quickly from the garden when you want him. It is far more important that your dog will recall where you need him to recall – out and about in public. In this section we bring you a step nearer to that goal as we begin to practise our new recall in some different locations.

Keeping it simple

As we take the basic recall you have taught your dog into new locations, we need to find ways to make these new practice exercises as simple as possible. We will not be involving other people or dogs at this point as each new location is, in itself, a distraction. This means keeping all other distractions to a minimum.

So, you are not going to head for the beach, release your dog, and then call him away from another strange dog just yet. Let's take it one step at a time.

Your first step is to decide on a number of different locations; places where you would like to be able to exercise your dog in the future and be confident that he will come back to you when you call him.

In each of your chosen locations we are going to:

- Avoid all unnecessary distractions

- Interact with the dog

- Set up recall exercises

- Practise, practise, practise

If you have had a lot of recall problems with your dog in the past, it can be helpful for these first outings to be in a place that is unfamiliar to him. You should certainly avoid any locations where you have previously had a serious problem. Taking him back to the scene of his crimes is asking for trouble as his memory of past events may override all the good work you have done up until now. If, for example, your dog ran away and was lost for three hours, or chased a deer across three fields last time you went there, then this particular location is not a good place for these initial outings.

Avoiding unnecessary distractions

The fact that you are asking your dog to recall in a completely different place is a big step for him. Don't make it harder by adding a load of temptations. Try to avoid surprises. When you first call your dog away from another dog in this new location we want it to be on your terms. You do not want to be taken unawares by a group of ramblers or a pack of dogs and have to attempt to recall the dog in a difficult situation that you have no control over.

You will need to give some thought now to how you are going to avoid distractions other than the ones you have chosen to train for in any given training situation. Typical distractions might be:

- Children playing, squealing or running about

- Footballs and Frisbees being thrown

- People and dogs splashing in water or swimming

- Bikes and joggers moving quickly

- Other dog walkers and their dogs

- Wild animals – rabbits, squirrels, birds etc.

- Fascinating (to the dog) smells on the ground (horses, rabbits etc.)

One way of avoiding powerful distractions, such as other people and dogs, is to visit your new locations at unsociable hours. If you know your dog loves bouncing up to strangers and pestering them for food and cuddles, don't train on the beach on a busy day. Go on a day, or at a time, when fewer people are about. This is easier to take advantage of in the summer when you can get out early before other dog walkers arrive. Failing that, choosing an open space where you can see people coming some way off is a good idea.

Wet weather is another good time to train without interruption. While everyone else is cowering at home, you can make good use of a rainy day by getting your waterproofs on and doing some training! Your dog won't mind the rain at all.

In rural areas it is easier to avoid distractions, with the possible exception of local wildlife. If your nearest training area is home to a large rabbit population, one option is to leave your dog in the car nearby or have a friend hold him while you have a stomp around in the area where you want to take the dog. If you cannot get any assistance, put your dog on a lead and walk all over the area where you will be training before you begin. Rabbits generally disappear underground for some time if you tramp about near their warrens. Of course the rabbit scent itself can be a powerful distraction, but it will be less challenging than the sight of a rabbit bobbing away into the distance.

If, despite your precautions, you get taken by surprise and your dog rushes up to a distraction, avoid using your new recall signal. If your dog approaches another person or dog, stay calm. Wander up and have a chat, and slip a lead on nonchalantly. Be nice to your dog and reward him generously as soon as you have him on his lead.

Plan, execute and leave!

Do not give the dog a meal just before his training session as he should be hungry. Take plenty of premium and basic rewards with you. If your dog is a recovering absconder you will need mega rewards. To start with you are going to reward every recall with premium rewards at the very least. The first couple of recalls will need the bonus treatment. Once you are successful you can start to reduce the frequency and quality of the rewards.

Think about each session with the dog in advance. Decide what you are hoping to achieve and think about the best ways to achieve that objective. Set up your session carefully. Do what you have to do, give yourself a pat on the back and go home. Don't be tempted to let the dog have a few extra minutes freedom or playtime if that will risk compromising your hard work. We are not trying to achieve obedience by exhausting the dog and there will be plenty of time for playtime when you have completed your recall training.

Keep your whistle in your mouth when your dog is off the lead. At any point where your dog volunteers a recall, i.e. when he rushes towards you simply because he wants to, you will blow the recall signal. This is building on your dog's conditioned response. If you have the whistle in your mouth at all times, then you won't miss any of these excellent opportunities. Of course you must not forget to reward these voluntary recalls too.

In between each exercise you need a period of time during which you and your dog engage in some kind of activity. This activity can be little bits of training using other skills such as 'sit' or 'down', or it can be a game such as 'tug' or fetching a ball. So before you set off make sure you have some toys with you. If your dog enjoys Frisbee, take one; if your dog likes to chase a ball, take one of those too. If your dog is intended for gundog work or you are interested in gundog training as a hobby then by all means take a retrieving dummy with you.

Engagement helps to keep your dog close and reduces the risk of self-rewarding. With some dogs, particularly those with pre-existing control issues, you will need the additional help of a training lead at this point.

Keeping a journal about your training is a good plan, especially at this stage when you are starting to train in new places and where you have far less control over what might happen. A training diary will show you just how far you have come and will help you get past any stumbling blocks.

Once you have blown the recall signal you must not blow it again. What you must do is everything in your power to get the dog to come back to you under his own steam.

Before you begin

When you arrive at your location, your first job is to check for distractions. If the coast is clear you can release the dog, but before you do, give him a tasty treat on the lead. You then need to be ready to engage with the dog. Start to walk along but aim to keep the dog close to you. Keep your whistle in your mouth and change direction at least every thirty yards.

If you are in an open field you can move around the four sides of an imaginary thirty-yard square. If you are confined to a track or path you will have to move to and fro. Do not set off in one direction and just keep going.

Think about the 'zone' we talked about in chapter six. As soon as the dog's attention starts to drift or he looks as though he is going to leave your zone of control, start to make yourself interesting. Make a noise, whoop, clap your hands, whatever you need to do. Throw a toy or kick a ball around on the ground. If, at any point, the dog charges right up to you, blow the recall signal (one time only) as he comes in and then reward him. Keep this interaction up for three or four minutes and then get ready to give a planned recall signal.

It is a good idea if you 'warm up' your dog at each new location with some very simple exercises that he can do right next to you. Ask him to sit while you step around him, walk a few paces with him on a loose lead and then ask him to sit again. Get him to 'sit and stay' while you step away and then return. These types of calm training exercises help to establish a working environment or atmosphere of cooperation between you at this new location. Spend a few minutes on these simple exercises before moving on to the following one. Do not be tempted to let him run around for half an hour to get rid of his excess energy.

Keep recall distance short to begin with

EXERCISE ONE **Come away from a loose dog**

By definition, a recall begins with the dog some distance away from you. We keep this distance very short to begin with but we cannot eliminate it altogether. In this first exercise we will encourage the dog to chase you as soon as the recall signal is given.

1. Let the dog get about five yards away

2. Check for distractions – do not call the dog if he is distracted

3. Turn your back on the dog, give the recall signal and run away

4. Look over your shoulder to check the dog is coming, turn to face him and as soon as he reaches you, pop him on a lead and reward him very generously

5. Release the dog and continue to walk for a couple of minutes

Behave just as you did when you first released the dog, keep changing direction and engaging with the dog. Carry on walking in this manner for a couple of minutes then:

6. Recall the dog again through steps 1 to 4. This time do not release the dog

7. Keep rewarding, petting, praising and fussing over the dog for a minute or two then walk on with the dog on a lead

This short period of lead walking serves several purposes. It gives you a break from concentrating on the dog and it gives you the chance to move to a slightly different part of your training location. When you have walked on a little way, release the dog and engage with him just as you did at the beginning. Now repeat the whole exercise in a different part of the field / wood / park.

What if he doesn't come back?

It is unlikely to happen but it is important to prepare for the possibility that your dog will simply ignore your whistle. If your dog ignores the recall you will need to take control and engineer a recall immediately to avoid any self-rewarding behaviour on the part of the dog. Do not be tempted to whistle again. We want an immediate response to a single command.

If the dog is wearing a training lead, step on it and give your no reward marker 'AH AH!' Now switch to fun mode, start your whooping and clapping or making silly noises. Whatever appeals to your dog. Run a few paces away and then crouch down and encourage the dog. If necessary, alternate running away and making yourself small and encouraging. Stop the dog with the long lead any time he tries to head away from you. Encourage and praise every step in your direction.

Do whatever it takes to attract your dog's attention but do NOT blow the whistle again. Keep running and whooping until the dog is heading your way, then crouch down and welcome him with open arms. Reward, reward and reward some more. Make him believe that changing his plans and coming after you was the best thing he did all week.

If your dog was not on a training lead, and you found it hard to get him to come to you, then you need to think about putting him on a training lead before you attempt any more recalls on location.

Every mistake your dog makes should be analysed and you should take steps to prevent a repeat performance. A single mistake will soon be forgotten. Two mistakes quickly become three, and three leads rapidly to a bad habit. Any time the dog fails to recall, ask yourself what you could have done differently.

What about slow responses?

Remember that if the dog dawdles on the way back and his recalls are slow and lacklustre you can fix this by selectively rewarding only faster recalls. So once you have had three or four successful recalls in a row, do not reward the next one unless it is a faster one. You will probably find that this increases his enthusiasm next time. You can do this at intervals, rewarding faster recalls and dropping the reward on slower ones. When you do this make sure that the recalls you do reward are rewarded generously.

Once you are able to get several nice fast responses in a row, where the dog comes straight in on your recall signal without you leaping about and making a spectacle of yourself, you can move on to exercise two. If you are working with a pup you might reach this point on your first outing; if you are working with a dog that has a history of recall problems it may take two or three trips to get there.

EXERCISE TWO **Long running recall**

This is just the same as exercise one except that you are going to let the dog get further away from you before you recall him.

1. Let the dog get fifteen to twenty yards away

2. Check for distractions – do not call the dog if he is distracted

3. Turn your back on the dog, give the recall signal and run away

4. Look over your shoulder to check the dog is coming, turn to face him and as soon as he reaches you, pop him on a lead and reward him very generously

5. Release the dog and continue walking for a couple of minutes

As before, interact and engage with the dog and keep changing direction. Carry on walking in this manner for a couple of minutes then:

6. Recall the dog again through steps 1 to 4. Do not release the dog

7. Keep rewarding, petting, praising and fussing over the dog for a minute or two then walk on with the dog on a lead

Release the dog for a bit more interactive walking before repeating. After several successful long running recalls, move on to exercise three.

EXERCISE THREE **Short standing recall**

The difference in this exercise is that you are going to remain still. You won't be giving your dog that extra sense of urgency he may feel when you whistle as you walk away. Note that we have decreased the gap between the two of you to make the exercise easier in this respect, because we are making the exercise harder by standing still. When you make one aspect of a training exercise harder, always make the other aspects easier to begin with.

1. Let the dog get about five yards away

2. Check for distractions – do not call the dog if he is distracted

3. Stand still and give the recall signal

4. As soon as the dog reaches you, pop him on a lead and reward him very generously

5. Release the dog

Carry on walking exactly as before for a couple of minutes then:

6. Recall the dog again through steps 1 to 4. This time do not release the dog

7. Keep rewarding, petting, praising and fussing over the dog for a minute or two then walk on with the dog on a lead for a while

Once you have had several successful fast recalls, increase the distances again.

EXERCISE FOUR **Longer standing recall**

Remember to break up the exercises with periods of interactive walking.

1. Let the dog get fifteen to twenty yards away

2. Check for distractions – do not call the dog if he is distracted

3. Stand still and give the recall signal

4. As soon as the dog reaches you, pop him on a lead and reward him very generously

5. Release the dog

Carry on walking, exactly as before, for a couple of minutes and then:

6. Recall the dog again through steps 1 to 4. This time do not release the dog

7. Keep rewarding, petting, praising and fussing over the dog for a minute or two and then walk on with the dog on a lead

Two man recall

If you have a friend with you, you can practise the two man recall at your new location. This is also a great way of giving the dog a bit more exercise under nicely controlled conditions. Don't forget you will need two whistles, and two bags of rewards, one for each of you. Start by calling the dog back and forth between you over just a few yards, gradually extending these distances. How far apart you go will depend on the size and fitness of your dog. Just make sure you don't compromise your ability to control those consequences.

Different locations

Once your dog is recalling well throughout a ten to twenty minute session (at the exercise four level), preferably on more than one visit, move to the next location on your list. Work through each of the exercises in this chapter at each location while avoiding distractions. We will introduce those in the next chapter. When you have covered all the locations on your list it is time to initiate the gambling effect.

Fading rewards

Now you will need to practise recalls of varying lengths while reducing the value and frequency of your rewards. Start by replacing some of the premium rewards with basic rewards, and then begin to include some recalls where the dog is not rewarded at all. Soon you can drop the premium rewards and just give basic rewards from time to time.

Remember that to trigger the gambling effect and get your dog addicted to recall rewards, they must be intermittent and highly unpredictable. Include the occasional jackpot (an unexpected bonus reward) for perfect results.

Before we move on to the next chapter, *Putting it All Together*, I think it would be a good idea for us to deal with the question of water.

Recalling from water

Some dogs are extremely attracted to water and swimming. Others are not interested in it, and if this applies to your dog, feel free to skip over this part.

It is not unusual to find a dog that recalls perfectly well on land but that refuses to come out of the water. It is therefore helpful at an early stage to teach your dog that the recall command applies while swimming as well as running around in a field.

Some dogs find it hard to leave water behind

Problems tend to arise because people underestimate the attraction of water and fail to reward the dog effectively for leaving it. They also tend to try and recall the dog from deep water right from the start.

To avoid problems around water, you should begin by practising your recall command around shallow streams and even large puddles. And use powerful rewards until the recall is well established. Choose your initial location with care, and go well prepared as you will be getting up close and personal with a soaking wet dog.

Initially you will be encouraging the dog to return by making off in the opposite direction, but then you will need to establish a recall with you in a stationary position. If the dog ignores you, you will need to go through the usual procedures for getting him right into your arms. Run away, turning at intervals to see if he is ready to greet you. Now take hold of him and reward him thoroughly, slowly and generously. The more you practise recalling from shallow water, the less likely your dog is to refuse a recall from deep water.

You can use a training lead in this shallow water exercise, but be aware that you won't be able to do so in deep water in case the lead tangles up on submerged roots or other obstacles. If you have had trouble getting your dog out of water in the past, you should go prepared with some mega rewards for this first exercise.

EXERCISE FIVE **Recall out of water**

1. Encourage your dog into a shallow stream.

2. Recall the dog from the bank walking away from him as soon as you have blown the whistle

3. Reward very generously when he returns, and let him go back into the water again

4. Repeat several times

Try not to recall the dog out of water just before taking him home, we don't want him to associate leaving the water with the end of all his fun.

The dog must be confident that coming out of the water is rewarding, and that you are the source of access to more water games.

The whole exercise needs to then be practised in a different location, still with shallow water. Only when the dog is really good at this exercise should you attempt to call him from deep water such as a lake, river or the sea.

Summary

Here is a summary of the approach you need to take when teaching your dog to recall in new locations:

- Check there are no distractions before releasing the dog

- In between recalls, engage the dog in activities

- Start with very short recalls (five yards max)

- Encourage the first couple of recalls at each new location by running as you call

- Increase the length of recalls gradually

- Fade rewards gradually

Try to look on this as a bit of an adventure. It makes a nice excuse to visit brand new walking locations too, though it is probably a good idea to have a look at the location without your dog in advance of taking him to train there. Keeping the dog 'engaged' with you in between recalls helps to ensure that he does not get into mischief, we are still building new habits here and we are aiming for success every time.

Remember that concentrating on your dog to this extent is quite demanding so give yourself a nice reward for all your efforts. Use lead walking to give yourself a break. Remember that there is no reason what-soever why a dog should run off-lead for the entire duration of a walk.

Can you answer the following questions now?

- Does you dog come when you call him at each of three different new locations?

- Does he come even when you stand still after blowing the whistle?

- Has he come reliably at least five times in a row on your most recent recalls?

- Have you been practising, on location, at least three times a week for at least two weeks?

- Have you faded rewards so that your dog is being rewarded intermittently?

Once you can answer yes to all of these questions it is time to make the big push. We are now going to bring everything you have learned together. We are going to take your new recall into the real world of distractions and unpredictable real life situations. Let's not waste any time. Let's move straight on to the next chapter, *Putting it All Together.*

CHAPTER 15

Putting it All Together

You and your dog are now entering the final stages of your journey. This is the part where we take the building blocks of skill that we have created and put them all together. There are a few more challenges ahead, but you are more than capable of overcoming them.

In this section you will take each of the locations where you are likely to walk your dog and work through the various distractions that he is likely to be tempted by. These could be distractions such as children playing, joggers running past or perhaps a walker with four dogs bounding along in front of her.

Planning

You will not able to control every aspect of when and where these distractions occur, though where possible you can set up fake scenarios first to teach your dog how to cope more easily with the real ones.

If you keep a checklist of each type of distraction that you are likely to meet, and the level at which it might occur, you will be able to keep track of your dog's progress and to better judge whether he is ready to cope with a recall in any given situation. You can see an example checklist overleaf. Make five columns and on the left hand side make a list of the different distractions you expect to come across during an average month in your local dog walking locations. In the next column note a couple of locations where you will be able to practise recalling your dog away from this kind of distraction. The remaining three columns can be labelled low, medium and high.

Low, medium and high levels of distraction

You can allocate levels to each distraction by looking at different criteria. If the distraction is a long way away, children playing Frisbee at the far side of a large recreation ground, for example, it is likely to be low level. If a squirrel shoots up a tree just two feet from your dog, however, that is a high-level distraction.

If the dog is very close to you that will help increase your influence over him and correspondingly decrease the influence of the distraction a little. A distraction twenty feet away from your dog might be a medium level distraction if he is standing next to you, but a high level distraction if you are twenty feet away from him.

Another important factor is what your distraction is doing. A boy sitting on a park bench playing with his mobile phone is not going to be as powerful a distraction as a boy kicking a ball about. Ultimately you will have to make a judgement as to the level that you allocate each distraction. This is not an exact science so don't worry too much about it. It is just a rough guide to help you build up your dog's ability to cope with distraction in a structured and effective manner.

Aim to get ticks for at least two locations in each of the low, medium and high columns for every distraction. A tick in the low box indicates that you can reliably recall your dog in the presence of the distraction listed on the left at the location named, where the distraction is at a low level. A tick in the medium box indicates you have recalled the dog where there is a distraction of medium intensity and a tick in the high box shows that you have recalled the dog in the most challenging conditions. When

Advanced Recall Proofing

DISTRACTION	LOCATION	Low	Med	High
Ramblers or groups of people out walking or hiking	Southham Forest	✓	✓	
	Wittams Farm	✓		
Children running around shouting and playing	Borewell Beach	✓		
	Rackley Park			
Dog walkers and off lead dogs	Borewell Beach	✓		
	Rackley Park			
Joggers / runners	Southham Forest			
	Rackley Park			
Wild birds seagulls / crows	Borewell Beach			
	Wittams Farm			
Wild animals such as rabbits or squirrels	Rackley Park			
	Wittams Farm			

you have put two ticks in each box you have completed the exercises in this chapter.

Look at each of your boxes and ask yourself if you can set up a planned fake distraction to practise with your dog under more controllable conditions. This will enable you to ensure that the dog gets to practise with low levels of the distraction before being exposed to an intense version of the same distraction.

Low-level distractions first

Obviously it is better for the dog if you can practise with distractions at low levels before moving on to the most challenging recalls of all. And while you cannot always arrange for this to happen naturally, in some cases you will be able to contrive a situation to help you continue this step-by-step proofing process.

Keep your dog closely supervised as you work through this process. The nearer you are to your dog, the more control you will have and the less likely you are to be taken unawares. If in doubt, have the dog drag a training lead for the next few weeks to give you that extra bit of control.

You are entering the world of advanced proofing now, so be kind to yourself if you slip up occasionally and reward the dog and yourself generously for your successes. To carry out this advanced proofing effectively you will need a consistent and effective recall proofing strategy.

Advanced recall proofing strategy

The following four criteria are the components of your recall proofing strategy, and they apply no matter what conditions you are proofing in or against.

- Define your objective

- Reduce other factors of difficulty

- Give strong cues – whistle plus departing handler

- Give big rewards each time you raise the bar

Define your objective

Before you start any training session you should be clear on what your objective for the day is. Are you getting your dog to recall away from seagulls? Are you expecting him to recall away from joggers? What is it you want the dog to do today?

It helps to pick one objective and stick with it, even though in the real world things do not always go smoothly. A back up plan is always a good idea. If you come across a load of mountain bikers where you were expecting rabbits, then you may just have to cope with the new scenario when it happens.

Reduce the level of difficulty

There are two key ways to reduce the level of difficulty for each recall. You can reduce the power of the distraction and you can reduce the length of the recall.

Remember, the power of the distraction will increase the closer the distraction is to the dog, and the more tempting and powerful it is. In many cases, diluting a distraction simply means moving further away from it. If you can practise releasing and recalling your dog repeatedly at a hundred yards away from where another dog is playing Frisbee, and then reduce that distance gradually, you are far more likely to be successful when you attempt to do the same thing from ten yards away.

One way of practising 'diluted distractions' like this is to get friends and relatives to set up fake scenarios like the ones you might meet in public places.

Take a friend with you and set up exercises just like the ones you did in your garden at home. For example, work through the three exercises in *Proofing with Dogs*.

- Come away from a dog

- Come away from a moving dog

- Come away from a loose dog

You can also pick one of the distractions on your list and set up a fake low-level version of it, using a friend to help you. To make the set up realistic, you and your friend may need to arrive at your chosen location separately. Arrange a mutually convenient time so that you can appear with your dog shortly after your friend has arrived. Pick a time when there are not too many other people around.

You could, for example, ask your friend to kick a ball around on your local recreation ground with her children while you approach from a distance. Take some premium rewards with you and if your dog has a history of recall problems have him drag a training lead.

Recall your dog frequently, as far away from your friend as possible, and then gradually move closer. It is a good idea to mix other simple exercises in between recalls, to keep the dog focused on you. Make him do a few sit-stays and play some games with him in between letting him run around. Aim to keep him 'in the zone'.

Circle your friend at thirty to forty yards away, all the while recalling and rewarding the dog at intervals. Use the training lead to stop the dog rushing towards your friend if necessary. If you have made big progress already today, with a distraction that your dog has struggled with in the past, don't be tempted to push your luck and go closer, especially if the dog is clearly taking an interest in the distraction. Stop while you are doing well and if the dog is having trouble focusing on you, move him further away from your friend until he can complete his recalls without any extra help and encouragement from you.

You can do exactly the same kind of fake set up to call your dog away from where a friend's dog is playing or being exercised. Again, arrange to arrive separately so that you can approach from a distance and practise far enough away for your dog to succeed repeatedly.

Of course you can, and should, do these types of exercises with genuine distractions at a distance, but to begin with you might feel more in control, and find it more helpful, if you set a few of them up in advance.

Remember that the recall starts with one whistle signal (pip-pip-pip-pip-pip) and ends when the dog reaches you for his reward. Your job is to make sure that these two events follow each other in rapid succession. When you can do this several times in a row, the dog has succeeded at that level and you can put a tick on your chart.

Recall training like this requires some effort, as you will need to watch the dog constantly. You may start to feel annoyed because you can't relax and enjoy yourself but just remind yourself how awful it felt to have a dog that wouldn't come back to you. It will be worth the effort to get the job done properly. This really is one of those situations where you get back what you put in. The more effort you make now, the more you will be able to trust your dog in the future.

I go on and on about big rewards and now is not the time to start skimping. Now is the time to pull out all the stops! We are talking big and tasty. This is even more crucial if you are training a dog with a previous history of recall problems.

Essentially, the bigger the challenge the bigger your rewards should be. As you make progress with each objective, you can diminish the rewards and replace them with sporadic tiny treats and the occasional jackpot. But do bring out the high-value rewards again when you start working on the next objective.

Set up practice exercises

Because your own situation is unique, you will have to design your own exercises from now on. You can do this. You might even find it helpful to write out the steps just as I have done in the exercises in the previous chapter. Take the example just given, of your friend playing football with her kids. You can break this down into the steps below.

1. Approach your assistant and the distraction that they are creating from a distance

2. Keep far enough away to avoid distracting the dog

3. Engage the dog in activities and keep him in the zone

4. Let the dog get 10 to 15 yards away from you and recall him

5. Reward your dog very generously

6. Move ten to fifteen yards closer to your assistant and repeat steps
    1 to 6

The initial distance between you and your assistant should be far enough that the dog is not unduly distracted. If at any time the dog becomes overly distracted by your assistant move further away, and as his focus on you improves, move closer.

This whole process can be set up again in different places. Sometimes you will be able to practise using situations that arise naturally and at other times you will need to get friends involved. But each time you practise your dog will improve. People are often surprised at just how effective this simple strategy – of creating some distance between a dog and a distraction – can be.

Taking control

Of course it is not always possible to rehearse every situation in this way. Sometimes you will be taken by surprise. When an unexpected distraction arises in a situation that you have not trained for, try to avoid using your new recall. Take control by using your strong cues (running away, whooping, clapping hands, whatever it takes) to help trigger the recall response in your dog. In any new or challenging situation, try to get the recall started like this before you give your whistle.

You need to be proactive in ensuring your good recall habit is not broken. Your job is to avoid recalling your dog in situations where the chances of him responding are poor, and to set up situations where you can practise the recall with the same distraction in a diluted form.

In situations where you can see trouble in the making, and cannot avoid it, put your dog on a lead and walk him past the distraction. Don't attempt a recall just to test him. Remember that the more times he recalls successfully because you have controlled the situation, the stronger the recall habit, and the more likely he will be to return without question when you need him to come back quickly in an emergency.

Anticipating problems

Any dog that has exhibited strong chasing behaviour in the past will need to wear a training line when you begin exposing him to his trigger situations again. Follow the instructions on accustoming the dog to the training line to reduce the chance of him becoming wise to the line. You can fade the training lead gradually by making it shorter and shorter over time, to make the transition to working without the lead.

If your dog is crazy about other dogs, it will help you greatly at this point to join a good group dog training class. The only way to practise recalling away from other dogs is to recall your dog away from other dogs. Although I have shown you how to set up this kind of scenario with a friend, there is no substitute for practising among lots of other dogs.

You may need to be discrete about rewarding the dog with food if other members of the class are not doing the same. Check with the trainer first that you are allowed to bring food to a training session. Some trainers do not allow this.

Keeping focused

It is very tempting not to take the trouble to dilute distractions, or to skip setting up fake training situations, especially if your dog has made really rapid progress so far. Introducing different challenges gradually may be thoroughly inconvenient. Yet crucially, one of the key differences between those that fail with recall training and those that succeed is a willingness to face the challenges involved in setting up carefully staged training opportunities for the dog.

It can be easy to falter at this point in your training; you want to enjoy a relaxing walk and don't want to give up hours of your time simply focusing on the specific needs of your dog. But remember what you stand to gain, and lose, depending on your progress.

Keep checking back on your list and aim to get at least two ticks in each box (working on low-level distractions first). Remind yourself that if you introduce powerful distractions in all their glory before your dog is ready for them, all of your hard work so far may be undone.

Remember... a dog that won't recall in public is never relaxing to be with. Hang on in there. Complete your proofing checklist thoroughly and for perfect results continue to practise in as many different situations as you can. All that remains as you come to the end of the proofing stage is to keep your dog's recall in tip-top condition with sensible management and a lifelong conditioning habit.

CHAPTER **16**

Recall for Life

Congratulations! In completing the advanced proofing process set out in the previous chapter, you have achieved what many dog owners never even attempt. Your dog now comes when he is called, reliably, and in a variety of different locations and situations. Now that you and your dog have completed the Total Recall training programme, let's look at how we can achieve this with a little bit of attention to:

- Conditioning
- Supervision
- Training reviews

Conditioning

You remember how we keep talking about the importance of conditioning the recall response? Of pairing the recall signal with the recall itself so that the association between the two becomes ever more powerful? This is now something that you can continue throughout your dog's life, and it really is easy to do.

Just make sure that at least two or three times a week you pick a moment when you see your dog dashing towards you all of his own accord, and blow that whistle. If the situation does not arise on its own, engineer it. Trigger his chase response just as you did during the training programme and then blow the whistle as he approaches. Make a huge fuss of him when he arrives and from time to time have a really special treat to give him when he reaches your side.

Supervision and control

Practice makes perfect, goes the saying, and dog training is no exception. But with some dogs, training is not quite enough. If you have a dog with strong hunting instincts, you will need to supervise him to some extent throughout his life. Without that supervision he is very likely to revert to his old ways.

Finding activities you can enjoy together will go a long way towards preventing a deterioration in behaviour, so do check out chapter twenty-three, *Getting Active with Your Dog*, for ideas and suggestions on getting involved in other activities that the two of you can share.

Remember, too, that dogs have great respect and fascination for anything and anyone that alleviates boredom. The more interesting you are, the more your dog will want to hang around with you.

Training reviews

Over the course of a few months you may find that your dog's recall response starts to get a little sloppy. If this happens, don't be tempted to ignore it or put it down to the weather or an off day. A sloppy recall is most usually a result of poor rewards and predictable boring behaviour on the part of the trainer. These are issues you will need to review if you are having problems. It is a good idea to take an objective look at your dog's training every few months and ask yourself if it needs any attention. Think about what you have been doing and make any necessary adjustments to your reward schedule and / or increase your level of interaction with your dog.

Over time, you can gradually swap food rewards for other types of reinforcement if you wish. This is especially easy to do if your dog enjoys retrieving. A really fast or difficult recall can be rewarded by a retrieve of a ball or toy. Don't forget it is only a reward if the dog rates it highly. A favourite reward for one of my cockers is to be allowed, on a signal from me, to jump into my arms. Not recommended when muddy!

Just remember that zero rewards results in extinction. Even the most obedient of dogs will still occasionally need a nice reward for completing a recall.

Novel situations

Of course you cannot train for every eventuality and from time to time you will find you need to recall your dog in a completely novel situation. If you have proofed your recall thoroughly, and conditioned it well, your dog will now be a recall junkie. He will be addicted to recall, compelled to come whenever he hears that whistle and overjoyed at the thought of rushing towards you. You will now find that your recall will hold up in almost any situation. This is partly because with thorough training we have gradually overcome the dog's poor ability to generalise the recall signal, and partly because the recall response has become such a strong habit that it is totally automatic in almost every situation you may come across.

I say 'almost' because there is always some distraction or disaster some-where that will overwhelm even the best trained dog. We cannot predict what a dog will do in extreme situations any more than we know how we will react ourselves. For this reason, it is vital that you never gamble your dog's life on his recall. Where railway lines, motorways, cliff edges or other dangers threaten, it goes without saying that you should always put the dog on a lead.

Further skills

In the same way that recall is about far more than just training, this train-ing system gives you far more than just a recall. The principles, techniques and strategies in this book can be put to work to teach your dog a whole range of other skills. I hope you will find the knowledge you have gained helpful and will put it to work to achieve a perfect response to other commands like 'sit' or 'down', and to teach your dog to walk nicely on a lead. Whatever you decide to teach your dog, you will be able to train and proof in easy steps using the rules of behavioural modification that you are now familiar with.

You can teach and proof the 'Down' command in just the same way as your recall

The bonding power of training

I hope that you have enjoyed working through this training programme and that you will spread the word about the importance of proofing in dog training.

A breakdown in recall is more than a breakdown in training, it is a breakdown in control. Recovering that control will transform your enjoyment of your dog and open a whole world of opportunities for you to enjoy together. Training a dog creates far more than a trained dog; it creates a unique bond or working relationship between the dog and his handler; it enhances and raises your status in the eyes of your dog; and puts you firmly in the position you want as a true leader.

The skills we have talked about here are quite basic ones. But many dogs are capable of far more. There are so many activities and pursuits that you can enjoy with a dog and you can read about these in the final part of this book. There is bound to be something that you can get involved with together and I hope you will give one of them a try.

PART **3**

Problem Solving

- Where Did I Go Wrong?

- Out of Control?

- The Absconder

- The About Turn Walk

- The Artful Dodger

- Using a Training Lead

- Getting Active with Your Dog

- The Finish

CHAPTER 17

Where Did I Go Wrong?

If your dog's recall is fairly poor, it is a good idea to go over what went wrong the first time around. By now you probably have a few ideas of your own, but it is important to clear up any misconceptions about what might have happened in order that we can move on and avoid repeating old mistakes.

Before we get right down to the root of the problem let's have a quick look at some doggy characteristics that people often think are the cause of their recall problems.

Common beliefs about recall failure

In many cases people either put their recall problems down to a phase the dog is going through or sheer naughtiness on the part of the dog. Linking problems to a phase the dog is going through is understandable because recall problems tend to arise at a fairly specific point in a dog's life – towards the end of the first year.

Most dog owners are initially successful at recall training their puppy. This early success is largely due to the dependent nature of puppies, which are reliant on their human companion for their security. The new puppy owner is often lulled into a false sense of security by the adoring attentions of his young friend. Recall problems tend to arise a little later as the dog is approaching the end of his first year and growing in confidence, perversely this is usually just as his human companion is losing enthusiasm for the task of dog training. Most people are bewildered and frustrated by this unravelling of their previously successful command.

If you successfully taught your dog a good recall when he was younger, or if you have trained a dog successfully before, you are likely to feel very frustrated when things start to go wrong the second time around.

The adolescent phase

I often hear from people who are struggling with a young dog towards his first birthday. Commonly the cracks in a previously effective recall begin to appear as the dog matures and loses his fear of separation from his owner. This is often at around nine to twelve months of age. This age-related disobedience is frequently and erroneously put down to a temporary excess of adolescent hormones.

If your dog is around this age, you may well have been advised by friends that he is now an adolescent or teenager. You may be told he is going through a phase and that he will grow out of it. However, this is most unlikely. Without further training, with a few exceptions, your problem will not resolve itself as your dog gets older; in fact, quite the reverse. The problem is likely to get a whole lot worse unless you take action immediately.

Dogs vary in temperament of course, and an individual dog's temperament does undergo some changes as maturity approaches. Most dogs become more confident and independent in the second half of their first year, for example. However, these changes do not go into reverse as the dog becomes fully mature. A dog that is confident and independent at eighteen months old will still be confident and independent at three years old, perhaps even more so. It is this confidence and independence, coupled with lack of effective training, that is likely to be at the root of your problems, not his hormones.

If you are still not convinced, bear in mind that experienced trainers do not suddenly get into difficulties with their adolescent dogs. Provided you follow this programme and manage your dog sensibly you are not likely to find your dog exhibiting behaviour that is the canine equivalent of hanging out on street corners, drinking too much or running up excessive mobile phone bills. Put simply, dogs that are appropriately trained and supervised do not exhibit unpleasant signs of adolescent rebellion.

Are some dogs more naughty than others?

Many owners believe quite strongly that their dog is simply more naughty than other dogs. The concept of naughtiness is rather misleading as it implies a deliberate act on the part of the dogs. Sometimes entire breeds of dog are consigned to the naughty bin. In most cases, the naughtiness is confined to particular situations or locations; the dog behaves angelically at other times, reinforcing his owner's belief that he is choosing to disobey this time.

For many owners, early recall training goes smoothly and problems do not begin to arise until the dog comes into contact with other dogs in public places. It is quite common for a dog to come back beautifully when there is no one else around, but as soon as another dog appears he runs off and is completely deaf to his owner's shouts and whistles. Sometimes he will even follow another dog's family all the way home or back to their vehicle, which is highly embarrassing as it seems to demonstrate how little he cares for his own family.

It is important to realise that this dog is not a callous and uncaring creature. He hasn't stopped liking his owner and is not bright enough to work out that he is in serious danger of getting lost or stolen. He is just a very sociable dog that likes other people and dogs a great deal. More importantly, he isn't actually naughty, and we will look at that a bit more closely in a moment.

The real reasons why recalls fail

So, if our adolescent young tearaway is not being naughty, and if his hormones are not responsible, what is the reason for the breakdown in this dog's previously reasonable recall? You have probably guessed that training errors are involved somewhere along the line. But that is not the whole story. A perfect recall response requires a combination of good management and good training.

Failure to supervise a dog effectively, combined with strong hunting or chasing instincts, tends to result in a complete loss of control, even where training standards are reasonable; we look at this in more detail in the following chapter, *Out of Control?*

For many dogs though, there is a more general and less catastrophic breakdown in recall over time. This is often largely due to errors in training.

Common recall training errors

Here is a summary of the most common recall training errors:

- The owner stops rewarding the dog

- The owner rewards the dog for bad behaviour

- The dog rewards himself for bad behaviour

- Rewards are badly timed

- Rewards are insufficiently valuable

- Recalls are punished

- The owner fails to proof the recall

Forgetting to reward good behaviour

Some recalls fail because the owner stops rewarding the dog. This is surprisingly common – partly because of the old myth that using food is cheating, and partly due to a lack of understanding about alternative rewards.

For the most part though, people just get sloppy. This is human nature. We are all inclined to take things for granted when they are working well. Recall is no different. You call, and the dog comes. All is well with the world. If you stop rewarding the recall, or reward it ineffectively, sooner or later the dog will try something new when you call, such as finishing his investigation of an interesting rabbit burrow, chasing a leaf or sitting down to have a little scratch. Most people vastly underestimate just how rewarding it is to a dog to simply run around in silly circles. And of course if the dog finds ignoring the recall rewarding, he will do it again and again.

Training a dog can be very stressful when things are not going well. The more the dog ignores the owner, the less likely the owner is to provide praise and reward because he is now worried sick about catching the dog and increasingly angry at his own inability to control him. When you are standing in the middle of a muddy field in the pouring rain, feeling thoroughly wound up by the antics of your dog, the last thing you are inclined to do is tell him how great he is when he eventually deigns to return. Yet praise him and reward him you must if you want him to return faster next time.

Rewarding bad behaviour

It is not unusual for dog owners to actually reward a refusal to recall. You might not think that you are rewarding your dog when he ignores your recall, but you may well be doing so inadvertently. This can be a particular problem with puppies and usually takes the form of the handler chasing after his dog. Dogs, especially young dogs, find being chased highly rewarding. It is one of the best games you can offer a puppy. Most young dogs find it completely thrilling to be pursued at speed around a garden or across the countryside. Like children, this enjoyment continues only up to a point. If you keep it up, and especially if you are clearly angry, the dog is likely to become frightened, but by then he has forgotten his misdemeanour and already discovered that you can't run very fast, and certainly not as fast as him, so you lose out either way. The best way to avoid recall failure caused in this way is to use sensible strategies when raising your puppy, and we look at those in our section on creating a solid puppy recall.

Difficulty preventing the dog from rewarding himself

Where a recall breaks down it is often because you are not the only source of rewards for your dog. There are some fantastic potential rewards that a dog can simply help himself to in the countryside, unless of course you take steps to prevent this happening. Chasing butterflies and galloping about annoying other dog walkers are rewarding to many dogs. And the chances are that your dog has been helping himself to these wonderful rewards directly after ignoring your recall.

Every time your dog chooses, of his own free will, to indulge in any activity that he finds amusing (chasing his tail or knocking toddlers over so that he can steal their ice-creams), he is self-rewarding. We all self-reward now and then, and it is often fine for your dog to do so when he is relaxing at home. Problems arise when the dog self-rewards immediately after bad behaviour. In this case the bad behaviour we particularly want to eradicate is ignoring the recall.

Another problem with self-rewarding is the fact that it devalues the owner in the eyes of the dog, and it devalues the rewards offered by the owner. If your dog can get better rewards away from you than he can get from you, then you are not really that special are you? Preventing your dog from getting his own rewards at a completely inappropriate time (i.e. when he has been bad) is crucial. This is just as important as remembering to reward the dog when he is good.

As training becomes more advanced, and we train in more challenging locations, it can be more difficult to control what happens immediately after your dog fails to respond to a recall. Every slip exposes the dog to more opportunities to self-reward in new and exotic ways, potentially leading to a spiralling loss of control. Once you have lost control of rewards, you need to regain control fast if you are to prevent things from deteriorating further.

The most simple way to reduce opportunities for your dog to self-reward outdoors is through the use of a training lead, and for any dog that is already in the habit of self-rewarding, a training lead is an essential aid. You can find a chapter about the proper use of training leads in the problem-solving section at the end of this book. Many dogs will need one when they begin practising their new recall outdoors.

Poor timing

Poor timing of rewards is a common cause of training failure. You call, the dog comes back, but you are busy chatting to your friend. If he hasn't already wandered off again you may notice the dog after a couple of minutes and rumple his ears. Even the most passionate ear-rumpling devotee will not feel rewarded for the recall if he completed it five minutes earlier. Poor timing of punishment is also common. Anyone choosing to correct a dog for failing to recall needs to do it at the time and place at which the dog disobeyed the command. With recall this is often impossible, because by definition a dog that disobeys a recall is usually some distance away.

Poor choice of consequence

A common cause of recall problems is poor choice of reward. Many dog owners understand that they should reward their dog for coming when he is called, but fail to view rewards through their dog's eyes. For a reward to affect future behaviour, we know that the reward must be valued by the animal being trained. However, to be effective as trainers, we also need to be in touch with what is actually valuable to dogs in general, and to our own dog in particular. For a lot of dogs, a pat on the head is the only reward they get for coming when they are called. It's hardly surprising that nine times out of ten, they really can't be bothered.

Remember that the value of the reward can only be assessed by the dog. You absolutely must get inside your dog's head and work out what he really likes best in the entire world. It could be sitting on your lap, fetching a ball or having his tummy tickled. You are in the best position to make this decision but you need to be objective and honest with yourself, because in the vast majority of cases, when studied by an objective observer, dogs will work harder for real food than anything else. By the way, your dog does not consider a dry biscuit to be real food.

Some dogs value human contact highly, many do not. If you are not sure how your dog feels about human contact (petting and stroking) as a reward, take him to a safe but unfamiliar open space and let him off the lead. After a couple of minutes, and when he is at least ten yards away, make sure he is watching you and sit down on the ground. If your dog rushes over to you and tries to climb on your head he probably places a high value on touching and physical contact. If, however, he takes one look at you, decides you have given up being in charge (you have after all made yourself small) and heads for the horizon, you will have a pretty good idea that charging around in a field is a lot more important to him than a stroke or a cuddle. You have no hope of training this dog with praise and affection alone. Even with the cuddly dog, food will be a tremendous asset in early recall training.

Punishing the recall

It is natural to feel angry when you are ignored. Many people pass that anger on to the dog when he eventually gets around to returning to them. How often have you seen a dog owner struggle to get his dog to come back and then give him a total ear-bashing when he eventually does: 'WHERE have you been you BAD DOG!'

The consequence for this recall was the application of a punishment! And as we now know, punishing any action on the part of the dog makes it less likely to happen in the future, so this trainer just significantly increased his chances of another failed recall.

Often, people call a dog to end their fun or spoil their game. It's time to go home and your dog is playing with next-door neighbour's puppy, and what do you do? You call him. If he comes to you, you then punish him by taking him home. Almost everyone makes this mistake at some point so don't be too hard on yourself if you have done this recently. Just make a mental note not to fall into this trap again. If you need to end your dog's fun – if you need to do something he might not enjoy – go and get him. Never use your precious recall command for this purpose. Bad things should not happen to your dog after a recall, especially during the training process.

Failure to proof the recall

There is a lot of information recall in the first part of this book and you are probably aware by now that a lack of proofing is by far the most common training error. If you need to review this information you can find it in chapter five, *All About Proofing*.

Don't forget that all of these different causes of recall failure will be subject to the influences of the temperament and past experiences of your dog.

Turning failure into success

The object of looking at all of these possible causes of failure is not to make you despair over the mistakes you have made, but to help you avoid making these mistakes in the future. There is a huge amount of conflicting information available on the subject of dog training and you are hardly to blame if you have made a few mistakes. Remember that every trainer, no matter how experienced, will mess up sometimes. The difference between those that are successful eventually and those that are not is that successful trainers learn from their mistakes and resolve to set the dog up to win next time.

In this chapter we have looked at the different causes of poor recall. But sometimes the problem is worse than that. Sometimes recall is virtually absent. In the next chapter we will look at a dog who is out of control and how things can be turned around to help him.

CHAPTER 18

Out of Control?

When your dog is making a complete fool out of you in a public place, apart from attempting to quell a distinct desire to strangle him, you are also probably wondering why everyone else's dogs are so irritatingly well behaved.

While we know that recall training is a matter of controlling consequences, this can be a greater challenge with some dogs than with others, especially when a dog has already started self-rewarding on a grand scale. Some of the most serious recall problems tend to arise in dogs that have very strong hunting and chasing instincts, or in dogs that have been rescued. It can be very lonely dealing with a difficult dog. The effects can be far-reaching and cause great distress to the dog's owners.

Take Helen and Rachel, for example. These two ladies both live on the same street in a market town in South West Surrey. Once a week after dropping their children off at school, they meet up to walk on one of Surrey's outstanding areas of heathland. They have been doing this for a couple of years, walking Helen's collie, seven-year-old Pippin. Rachel decided to wait until her youngest was at school before getting her first dog, a much longed for and loved Springer Spaniel called Joey, who at six-months-old began joining the two women on their weekday walks.

Pippin isn't perfect; to be honest she smells a bit, makes choking noises while dragging Helen along on the lead and yaps while waiting for Helen to throw a stick. But for the most part she is no trouble. Once her lead is off, she trots a few yards in front of the two friends while they chat and catch up on each other's news.

But just lately things have been a little strained. Joey has been running further and further away during walks, ignoring Rachel's calls, and several times he has disappeared for over twenty minutes. The second time he came back with a nasty cut on his leg and covered in mud. Judging from the quacking and flapping wings on the other side of the wood, Rachel was fairly sure he had been chasing ducks. Even more worrying was the last time, when Pippin followed Joey and was gone for five minutes, which isn't like her at all.

Rachel bought a whistle and taught Joey to come to it at home, but he completely ignores her outside. She also had him castrated a couple of months ago, but that has not made any difference. Lately Helen has been making excuses not to walk with Rachel, who is now increasingly nervous about letting Joey off the lead. Sometimes she doesn't let him off outside for several days at a time and he has started behaving badly at home, too. He has messed on the floor a couple of times because he doesn't like relieving himself on the lead, and he races around the house all day bouncing off the furniture and knocking things over. When Rachel shuts him in his crate, which she does more often now, Joey sometimes chews his feet until they bleed, which means a trip to the vet that Rachel can ill afford. Rachel loves Joey very much, but she works in the afternoons, has three young children to care for and Joey is rapidly becoming a burden.

The walks with Helen and Pippin had been a source of pleasure and relaxation to Rachel and now that is gone. She has not only been deprived of the dog she dreamed about owning for so long, she has also lost her weekly break with a friend and gained an extra and increasingly unwelcome responsibility into the bargain.

Hunting instincts

The problem with Joey is that he is a working bred gundog that has learned to self-reward in a big way. His breeding means that he is packed full of hunting instincts and this, in turn, means that hunting is in itself a massively rewarding experience. Joey's breeding needn't be a problem if he is managed the right way; but very often in pet homes, working spaniels are not sufficiently supervised outdoors to avoid problems arising. Indeed, one of the most common problems faced by many dog owners, especially those in rural areas, is a dog that hunts and chases wild animals. These

Working bred springers have powerful hunting instincts

dogs are not all gundog breeds, other breeds hunt and chase too, and some gundogs don't do either. There are no guarantees. Just be aware that if your heart sinks every time your dog takes off after a rabbit or a squirrel, totally deaf to your whistles and shouts, you are not alone.

You will have gathered by this point in the book that recalling a dog under such circumstances is an extremely advanced skill. It is pointless to attempt to recall a dog in hot pursuit of a moving object unless you have trained for it. And training for it is not necessarily the answer. Even working gundogs that are in contact with live game animals on a regular basis are not normally expected to recall during a chase. They are trained not to chase in the first place unless specifically instructed to find, and catch, a wounded animal. All that drive and enthusiasm is harnessed and then released in a controlled way to power the dog when required to hunt and retrieve through difficult terrain and seemingly impenetrable undergrowth.

Consequences again

Joey is learning through the consequences of his actions that exciting things happen when he gets far away from Helen and Rachel. When he follows the trail of a rabbit through the undergrowth, if he runs fast enough, he will catch up with the rabbit and can force it out into the open. The consequences are that a rabbit bursts out of the bush and flashes away inches from Joey's nose; what joy and delirious pleasures are provided by the ensuing chase.

At the same time Joey is puzzled and disappointed by Rachel's complete lack of interest in his favourite pastime. What is wrong with her?

What is the outlook for Joey?

Retraining a dog like Joey to recall in open country can be done, but it takes time. Rachel may need to allow months, not weeks, to effect a permanent change. In the meantime Rachel will need to stop allowing Joey to run free in the countryside where he would continue to self-reward through hunting; she will have to find other ways to exercise him and to stimulate his mind. Somehow she needs to prove to Joey that she is not a poor excuse for a hunting partner, but a fascinating person who can provide him with fun.

This is no easy task for a busy working mother. But Rachel is determined and has already made a start on retraining Joey with a brand new recall command. She has also booked Joey on some gundog training classes so that she can harness all that spaniel enthusiasm into retrieving and obedience exercises. And she has discovered that his obsession for chasing tennis balls can be turned to her advantage – she is now using ball play as an important reward for Joey in their training time together.

However, the sad fact is that many spaniels like Joey end up in rescue homes suffering from obsessive behaviours and sometimes self-mutilation. The families they leave behind them are often scarred by the experience and the guilt they feel from the rehoming process. But it needn't be this way. The best way to avoid Rachel and Joey's problems from the start is through proper management and training. Dogs that are hard-wired to hunt and chase need special care in this respect.

Why do some dogs chase?

So how is it that your friend's dog trots along happily all day at her heels while yours takes off after the smallest moving object? Well, much of it is down to genes. It is fairly obvious to most people that sighthounds such as salukis, whippets, borzois and greyhounds have an inbuilt urge to chase a moving object, but people are often surprised at the extent of this instinct in gundogs and other breeds.

Many of the most charming and placid pet dogs still have some of their hunting and chasing instincts intact. They are so much a part of our lives that we often forget that dogs are descended from formidable predators. While dogs have been domesticated for many thousands of years, they still retain many of the predatory instincts and skills that wolves or hunting dogs must have in order to survive in the wild

The rabbits and squirrels that are so numerous in the British country-side are an attractive and natural prey object to a dog. A powerful chase instinct with lightning responses and reflexes is the only way a dog in the wild is likely to catch one of these nimble animals. While some domestic dogs have lost these reflex urges, we have been breeding others to deliberately seek prey animals and to chase moving objects; such is the case with our working gundogs and racing dogs.

Gundog instincts

As Rachel has now discovered, lurking beneath the charming exterior of many a spaniel and quite a few retrievers, there often lies a determination to pursue and capture other live animals; this can shock owners and causes a lot of unexpected heartache.

The gundog category dominates the pet dog market in the UK. Out of the top ten breeds registered in Britain in 2010 almost two-thirds (including the top three) were gundog breeds.

Many people assume that all gundogs are biddable by nature and to an extent this is true. But in some working lines, hunting drive is so strong that this tends to overwhelm the dog's inclination to cooperate if not harnessed from an early age. Unlimited access to excessive rewards will always convince this dog that his owner is simply incapable of offering anything in the way of interesting guidance or partnership.

Owning a non-gundog breed is no guarantee that your dog will not become an inveterate squirrel chaser. There are many other breeds of dog that love to chase anything that moves, and several of these breeds lack some of the cooperative tendencies of many gundogs. At least your spaniel wants to play ball with you – your terrier probably wants to keep it for himself! So what can we do about dogs that become uncontrollable as soon as they are let out into the countryside?

Avoiding trouble

One of the best ways to prevent a chasing problem developing is to make sure it never gets established. The first few times a dog chases a rabbit or a squirrel will be quite half-hearted. He is inexperienced and his hunting instinct is not fully awakened. However, it does not take many chases before the dog with a strong chasing instinct is completely switched on to the pursuit. Your main opportunity for prevention is before he gets to this point and this means managing and supervising your dog when he is off the lead. There is more information about this kind of managed exercise in chapter six, *Beyond Training*.

What about a cure?

Once a dog has actively learnt to enjoy chasing wild animals, retraining him is not a straightforward process. Your best chance of success is to learn to keep your dog within a few yards of you at all times and keep him occupied. Spaniels can be taught to hunt from side to side in front of you looking for tennis balls that you have hidden in the grass. And I highly recommend gundog training classes for young spaniels as these provide activities that spaniels enjoy such as retrieving and quartering. All dogs can, and should, be taught to retrieve, especially chasers as this allows them to indulge their instincts in a safe and controlled manner. There are also games you can play to teach a dog to break away after a ball or toy during a chase (see the chase recall on the following page).

Once you have the dog interested in you and committed to interacting with you in some way (with ball games, for example) you can begin introducing these games and activities in increasing proximity to whatever triggers your dog's desire to chase. You will need to do this in the same way as described in the training programme – with the chase object initially at a great distance and gradually brought closer. Of course this is easier to set up if your dog chases joggers or cyclists than it is if he chases deer, because you can get friends to help you set up fake training situations. There is no 'one size fits all' solution and you will need to work around your own circumstances and the unique temperament of your dog.

Increased supervision

For most people, supervising a chaser of whatever breed, and maintaining a tight zone of control, will be an essential accompaniment to training a new recall command.

People sometimes find this difficult to accept. They want their rabbit chaser to stop chasing, but they do not want to stop him from running off-lead where there are lots of rabbits to chase. I am afraid there are no magic solutions to this one: if you won't supervise the dog, you won't be able to stop him chasing wildlife.

Remember that to control behaviour you have to control its consequences. This is your first step and without it, success is unlikely.

Regaining control

When dog owners like Rachel seek help they are sometimes disappointed to discover that they need to make significant changes to the way in which they exercise their dogs in order to succeed with their training. In a few cases the family concerned are not prepared to change their walking habits or the way in which they manage their dogs, often leading to the dog being rehomed. However, I have also seen many success stories. These successes are down to the owner's commitment to training; their willingness to reconsider the way they manage their dog's time off lead; and in some cases their enthusiasm for getting involved in activities such as agility or gundog training.

If you have lost control of your dog, take advantage of this chance to rethink how you supervise your dog. For this type of dog, the temporary use of a training lead is likely to be essential. Read up on how to use a training lead; review the information in Part One on managed exercise; start working your way through the training programme in Part Two; find some games and activities that you and your dog can enjoy together; and teach him to use retrieving or ball games to give him lots of cardiovascular exercise.

Chase recall

For dogs other than working gundogs, one useful game you can play that involves a chaser is to throw a ball or toy to a friend (ensuring that the friend is nimble enough to catch or step on the ball) and let your dog run after the ball as you throw to your friend. Call the dog by name during the chase. He won't respond to start with, and will probably pester your friend for a bit, but bide your time. When he gives up and looks in your direction, throw a different toy in the opposite direction from the first, so that he has to run right past you to chase after it.

As you repeat the game, the dog will begin to grasp that if he does not pay attention when you call, he doesn't get to have the ball or toy that he was chasing. Only when he starts to pay attention to you should he get some more fun. Sometimes you will need to throw the first ball in the direction of your friend and let the dog get it, making sure you do not call him on these occasions. If you don't occasionally let him get the ball he may stop bothering to chase it altogether.

After several repetitions of this game the dog will start to respond to your call sooner, and before long will be spinning around before he even reaches your friend. As the game progresses, you can gradually delay your throwing of the second toy until the dog has actually come back to you, but to begin with throw it as soon as he pays you any attention. When you can call the dog back and get hold of him before throwing the second toy, you can start using your recall whistle during the chase. Follow the whistle with his name the first few times and you will find he will soon respond to the whistle alone.

This is one more way of teaching the dog that good things come from you, but it is also good practice for him in that he is learning to break off his chase and turn at speed back towards you. Incidentally, we don't normally use this game with working gundogs because we want them to sit or remain at heel when they see a dummy thrown or a rabbit run past.

This game won't guarantee you a recall when your dog takes off after a rabbit, and you should not use your recall in such a situation if you have any doubt that the dog will obey. But, if your dog is ever in danger while chasing anything or running at speed, and you need to get him back, having had regular practice at this game will give you a much better chance of success. Do remember that with any chasing behaviour, the most important step you can take is to put a stop to all opportunities for your dog to chase before you begin retraining the recall.

When you have had control issues with a dog, make good use of the training lead as you work through the training programme in Part Two. Don't be in too much of a hurry to leave the training lead behind. Once they are closely supervised and properly rewarded, most dogs make rapid progress with their new recall. But remember, old habits die hard. Give it three months before trying any recalls without the lead, and stick to the order of progression in your training programme. Stay away from places where your dog previously got into trouble for six months. Take it slowly. It probably took a year or so to get him into trouble, it may take several months to install a good recall.

CHAPTER 19

The Absconder

I t is infuriating to have to wait in the middle of a woodland track, or stand sheepishly in the park, empty lead in hand and throat sore from shouting while your dog gallivants about with someone else's puppy or steals crisps from indignant children. It is quite another matter to realise that your dog is not only ignoring your whistle, but that he actually has no intention of returning at all.

While many dogs have recall problems, the vast majority have no desire to leave home. Plenty of dogs are sloppy about coming when they are called and ignore their owners' pleas to return when they are playing with other dogs. Many a dog will embarrass his owner by jumping all over a complete stranger instead of responding to his whistle. But at the end of the day, and at the end of each walk, the average dog wants to go home with his family.

However, for a small proportion of dogs this is not the case. Sometimes a dog will run off when he is let off his lead, and keep running, with no intention of coming back; at least not in the near future. In the majority of cases, this problem arises when an adult dog has been placed with a new family. It is very uncommon in dogs that have been with the same family since puppyhood.

What makes an absconder?

Absconding is a serious and very distressing problem. An absconder has learnt that being with people is no fun at all, and that being free – running around and pleasing himself – is the best experience in the world. As many absconders are rescue dogs, it is not always possible to determine how their bad habits originated. Some people do punish the recall by remonstrating with a dog when he returns after chasing squirrels or playing with other dogs, and if this happens repeatedly a dog may become very reluctant to return to the owner at all.

Some rescue dogs have just been generally abused or neglected and have come to the conclusion that people are no fun. Many rescue dogs have simply never formed a deep enough bond with a human being to want to go home with them at the end of a walk. The good news is that you can usually change this sad state of affairs. The bad news is that it can take a long time to do.

Tackling the problem

Living with an absconder is not easy. You will need to decide whether you would prefer to deal with the problem by keeping the dog permanently restrained in public, or whether you would like to try to attempt a cure. Success is not guaranteed, but in most cases even the most determined absconder can be trained to recall. It will, however, take months rather than weeks. Treating a serious 'running away' problem needs a three-pronged approach. It requires that you:

- Ensure the dog's safety

- Build a strong bond between you and the dog

- Thoroughly retrain the recall using exceptional rewards

Safety first

Safety is a big issue with an absconder. Owners of these dogs are sometimes overly optimistic. They will let the dog off the lead in a public open space on numerous occasions, despite the fact that he has disappeared from them for hours and even days at a time in the past.

It should be emphasised that if your dog has absconded before, he is likely to again unless he has been extensively retrained. I appreciate that you are concerned that your dog's exercise needs should be met, but safety must come first. This dog must not be let off the lead unless he is in an enclosure, and until you have made some significant changes. You will need to build a good relationship with the dog and to start working your way through the Recall Training Programme in Part Two. The difference in your case is that for a considerable time you will have the dog attached to a training lead while working on his training outdoors. Initially you will also need to keep hold of the end of the training lead rather than letting it drag along the ground.

What about exercise?

As far as exercise is concerned, the dog will not come to any harm through lack of exercise in the short term, provided that you have a safe garden or access to another similar enclosure where he can stretch his legs, chase a ball, etc. If you can walk him on the lead for half an hour, twice a day, even better. In open spaces he can also be exercised on a training lead. The daily exercise requirements of dogs are sometimes overstated. No dog needs to run the length and breadth of the county each day in order to remain healthy; nor will exercise wear him out so that he becomes more biddable. Trainers that focus extensively on exhausting a dog in order to gain some control over him often omit to mention that the dog's capacity for stamina is much higher than that of the average human being. The more exercise your dog gets, the fitter he will become and the further you will need to walk to tire him out next time. Unless your hobby is marathon running, you are unlikely to win at this game!

Absconders can be exercised on a long line

Building a bond

Most absconders have never formed a significant bond with a human being, and it is very important that the absconding dog builds a meaningful relationship with at least one member of his family. Just like people, dogs take time to get to know new family members and to grow to care about them. The fact that the dog is friendly towards you by the end of your first week together does not mean that he cares deeply about you, any more than the fact that you have laugh with the postman means that you want to jump in his van and go home with him.

If you brought a rescue dog home last week and he seems at home already, that's great. But you still have a way to go before he truly becomes a member of your family. The chances are that your rescue society will have forewarned you if your new dog has a history of absconding. Whether or not this is the case, introducing freedom to a rescued or adopted dog needs to be done with care.

Strategies for building a bond with a dog include:

- Relaxing together

- Hand feeding

- Getting active together

Dogs are highly social. Even when relaxing, they enjoy being close to other members of the family. Spending time with your dog, letting him sleep near you while you watch TV, grooming him and stroking him all help to establish a relationship. Some dogs will respond more quickly to this process if the bond is initially established with just one member of the family. It is therefore probably a good idea if you can make a particular effort to spend quiet time with your new dog in his first few weeks in your home.

Providing food

Food is a primary reinforcer. That is to say it has more value to the dog than most other forms of reward. With the absconder, every opportunity should be taken to reward the dog when he behaves in a desirable way, and food is usually the best way to do this.

While it is very nice for a dog to have a substantial supper to look forward to, with this dog your priorities lie elsewhere. You will be using every scrap of food your dog eats to shape new and better habits, and to build a clear picture in your dog's mind of you as the provider of good things.

Hand feeding

The absconder should be encouraged to earn much of their food, and every morsel should come from your hands. He needs to know that giving you what you want is the best way to get what he wants. Hand feeding is a great way to really get to know your dog and spend time with him. Divide his daily rations into lots of small portions; if he is fed on kibble this is easy; if he is fed on raw meat then you will need to wrap little portions in food bags and refrigerate them. Make sure they are easy to grab so that you can pop a bag in your pocket whenever you have time to go and do some training. You don't need to make a big deal out of training sessions, and it doesn't just have to be about recall. Teach him simple skills like 'sit' and 'down'. Reward him generously and lingeringly from your hands.

There is actually no practical reason why your dog should eat his food all in one go at mealtimes. Food is your friend and your tool; do not waste this precious resource by spending it all at once.

Getting active together

It is very important with this dog that you throw everything you have got into building a bond between the two of you and one of the best ways of doing that is by getting active together. Dogs get active with other dogs by going hunting together, and we substitute this activity with long country walks. However, with the absconder you simply cannot afford to risk him running loose in the countryside so you really need to find some activities that you can enjoy together where he is safe.

Find an enclosure where he can safely run around (a fenced garden or paddock) and teach him to retrieve. This will be a real help to you later, when you begin letting him run around freely outdoors again. You may be able to find an outdoor training class that takes place in a secure area; this will give you the added input of experienced advice from a professional trainer.

Retraining the recall

Before you can begin a programme of managed exercise with your absconder you will need to thoroughly retrain the recall command. As you work through the retraining programme in this book you will need to take some extra precautions. All outdoor training sessions that take place outside a safe enclosure will need to take place with your dog wearing a long training lead. In normal use a training lead is allowed to trail along the ground; with the absconder you will need to allow an additional period where you actually hold on to the other end of the lead during training sessions. At the end of this period you will begin to allow the lead to trail on the ground for short selected periods of time. When you have worked through each exercise in the programme, with the dog attached to a trailing training lead, you will then begin training for very brief periods, in each location, without the lead. A dog with a serious absconding problem may need to wear a training lead outdoors for a year or so before it is safe to begin working without one.

Do read through the chapter on using a training lead before attaching one to your dog. There are safety precautions you need to take and procedures you need to follow to ensure that the use of the lead is an effective aid in your training.

Removing the training lead

The first time you unclip the absconder's training lead you will need to take some precautions.

- Starve the dog for 24 hours first

- Avoid 'crime' scenes

- Have some exceptional rewards with you

- Increase off-lead time very gradually

- Avoid corrections

Starve the dog

That sounds so unkind, but we are talking about 24 hours, or one day and night – it is nothing really. Your dog will survive; his tummy may rumble a bit but we need him hungry!

Avoid the scene of the crime

There will be places where your absconder has led you a merry dance; places where he knows just how to have fun and how to give his human friends the slip; places that he will not have forgotten even if months have gone past. Think about the places your dog most often ran away. Was it on the moors? Was it on the beach? Avoid these places until you have confirmed his recall in many other less memorable places.

The longer you go without an absconding episode as you retrain your dog, the less likely it is that your dog will abscond again.

Exceptional rewards

Now is the time to go overboard with rewards. I am not just talking about your average jackpot reward. This is not the time for a sardine, or even a pouch of cat food. We are talking mega rewards here. Large quantities of hot (not burning) freshly roasted meat will hit the spot. Roast chicken and roast gammon are good choices. You can keep a whole roast chicken warm in foil and newspaper for quite some time and it smells absolutely tantalising to any dog. Pull big chunks of it off the bone to feed to the dog when you are ready. Warning: DO NOT FEED COOKED BONES! If you haven't had time to cook it yourself, you can buy 'ready to eat' hot roast meats in supermarkets. The idea is to provide the dog with something so special that he won't forget it for a long while.

This stage is not going to last forever and you will be able to return to simple and infrequent rewards eventually, but for now you are working on the most important transition in your training – the transition from being attached to a long line to running free. This is where there is huge

Big problems require big solutions. Keep warm in foil, but do not feed the bones!

potential for both failure and success and you have to make sure that the dice falls in your favour.

Increase off-lead time gradually

When you work through the training programme without the training lead, keep your sessions in each new location very short. If you have had to drive any distance to get there it will be tempting to overdo it and push your luck. Don't do this. Remember that this was once a dog that was very good at giving you the slip. At any moment something may happen to reawaken a memory of the kind of dog he used to be. You need to build up a new reservoir of good memories in each new location. Memories of happy recalls and games together, to replace the old bad habits, and this takes time and patience.

Obviously if you have had to drive some way, you may want to make the most of your time there; you can still do this by walking the dog at heel on a lead.

Avoiding corrections

Many absconders have been heavily punished in the past. They are usually extremely good at evading capture and may be very resilient to pain or discomfort. Don't be tempted to try and punish this type of dog; it will probably not work and may set you right back to square one.

Your job is to build a relationship based on trust. This dog needs to believe in your good intentions and to know that being with you will always be rewarding and enjoyable.

Summary

Safety has to be your prime concern for this dog; building a real bond together is very important. Working your way through the training programme using exceptional rewards will take time, but you will get there eventually. When you have reintroduced your dog to free running exercise be very careful to supervise him at all times.

In order to prevent your dog slipping back into his old ways you will need to keep in very close contact with him outdoors. Remember to establish a 'zone of control' outside of which your dog must not stray, and do whatever is needed to keep him happily occupied within the zone.

Your efforts will be rewarded. Be patient and allow several months for your retraining to take effect. Curing a serious recall problem is a tremendous achievement. You will never forget or regret the time you spend claiming control over your dog and enabling him to run free in safety.

CHAPTER 20

The About Turn Walk

For many dog owners, the daily walk is sacrosanct. It is something they feel they must do; it is part of their routine and essential for the welfare of the dog. It is also one of the key reasons that they bought a dog in the first place, it provides a daily escape from the stress and chores at home and an opportunity to relax and take in some fresh air and nice views. Of course the dog may see the walk in quite a different light.

The chances are that your dog views a walk as something of a hunting expedition. After all, this is what dogs do best; they run along together, comrades in arms, mile after mile, looking for food and adventure. And while most pet dogs have a square meal in their bellies at regular intervals, the instinct to run and hunt is often still strong.

For some dog owners these different agendas can lead to a sloppy or absent recall, and the loss of much pleasure from the once eagerly anticipated daily walk. The technique in this chapter is ideal for restoring a good recall in a dog that has just become a bit sloppy in responding to the recall while out on a walk. It is not a way to teach a dog a recall from scratch, or a way to deal with a dog that runs away when you take off his lead.

Your typical walk

If you own an active dog in good health you will probably find that your dog falls into a habit of running ahead of you on walks. He will return at intervals to 'check-in', and then rush off ahead again in a sort of forward and backward pattern. As your dog becomes more mature and independent, the distance he travels forward may increase, and the frequency of his check-ins may diminish.

Does it matter?

These increasing distances between you and your dog do matter, for several reasons. Firstly, in all but the most open terrain, the dog is likely to be increasingly out of your sight for significant amounts of time. Distance between a dog and his handler erodes control, and recalling your dog from long distances is a skill you need to train for and build up to. A dog out of sight is often out of control, and may get himself into danger.

Just as importantly, this behaviour is weakening the bond between the dog and you. Communal running is a team-building behaviour, travelling two hundred yards apart is not. And if your dog is not next to you or interacting with you in some way, the bond between you will lessen. Usually the owner finds that this increasing distance between them during the walk is accompanied by deterioration in recall. The dog comes back less willingly when you call him, often delaying his return or stopping off along the way to cock his leg or investigate a leaf.

Why do dogs run ahead?

The reason that dogs run ahead in the first place is simply that people do not usually keep up a pace that is comfortable for a dog. Many dogs do not like walking. Running is their thing. Unless you are running too, a dog's natural cruising speed is far greater than the pace you are travelling at.

Once the habit of running ahead has been formed, the dog quite naturally concludes that you are not much of a hunter and assumes that if anyone is going to find anything interesting on this hunt, it will have to be him. You, after all, are behaving like a weak or injured dog, and therefore it's up to him to take charge of the expedition. You will just have to keep up and follow along as best you can. And to be fair to him, he still thoughtfully checks back from time to time to make sure that you are OK.

Your behaviour deepens the problem

When you take your dog for a walk you will, in all likelihood, set off in one direction and keep walking in that direction for some time. Overall you probably walk in a large circle to eventually arrive back where you started. But at any one time, to all intents and purposes, you are walking in a relatively straight line.

This is great news for the dog as it means he knows exactly where to find you. Plodding along behind him at a snail's pace. This makes him feel very safe. He is free to run and explore ever further ahead without any danger of losing a member of the family.

If your dog is now effectively leading all your walks, and leaving you with the responsibility of following him, we can change that by making some simple changes to the way in which you walk. We are going to turn the tables on your dog and make him responsible for following you.

Making the dog responsible

Giving your dog the responsibility for finding you is a very effective strategy, but it does mean that you will initially have to behave rather oddly. I recommend you carry out this technique on your own, as it will drive anyone with you mad. Even a willing companion is not a good idea as you are likely to get absorbed in chatting to them and forget to follow the technique effectively.

Essentially, you are going to repeatedly change direction until the dog learns to pay close attention to where you are. Before you start you will need to prepare some food rewards to carry with you on each walk.

Method

Take your dog out to one of your normal walking areas, where you can safely release him without risk of him running onto a road. It is a good idea to avoid busy times when there are lots of other walkers about. Have the dog on a lead to begin with.

Stage one: stop calling

The first stage is very simple. Stop calling your dog!

Every time you recall a dog in a situation where he is unlikely to come, or where his return is likely to be sloppy, you are building a very bad habit and teaching him to ignore the recall. So for now, stop calling the dog.

Stage two: release the dog

Take the lead off your dog and release him. Take two steps forward to deceive him into believing you are behaving in your normal predictable boring fashion and then, as soon as he sets off ahead of you, make an about turn 180 degrees and set off in the opposite direction from that taken by the dog.

Do not look back, and do not make a sound. Just keep walking as fast as you can away from the dog. After a while, your dog will return to where he expects you to be. When he discovers that you are not plodding along behind him, he will be a little surprised and will come after you. Don't worry about him being able to find you; he will simply follow your scent.

Before long you will hear him panting and dashing up behind you. In all probability he will just assume that you made a somewhat unusual decision to walk in a different direction this morning, and will shoot straight past you with what he imagines are your new coordinates in mind.

Stage three: turn again

As your dog rushes past you, do an immediate about turn and set off briskly in the opposite direction to the dog. In other words, the same direction you were walking in a short while ago. Do not call the dog!

After a while your dog will check back and discover that once more you have changed your mind. This time as he rushes up from behind and shoots past you, you may notice the tiniest loss of power as he accelerates away in front of you. You have sown the seed of doubt in his mind. Supposing you change direction again?

Repeat this behaviour until the dog starts to slow down. Each time the dog shoots past you, turn on your heel and head the other way with all the speed you can muster. Do not call the dog at any point. All we are trying to do at this point is let the dog understand that you are becoming seriously unpredictable and that he needs to keep an eye on you at all times.

◄ Opposite *Please stop calling!*

Stage four: recall conditioning

Once the dog is approaching you more slowly from behind you can turn to face him and give your usual recall signal just before he reaches you. Make sure he touches your hand with his nose, reward him generously with some treats and tell him how clever he is to keep finding you. Send him off ahead of you again and then... about turn and set off in the opposite direction!

Do not be tempted to follow your dog at any point during the walk, and do not give the recall signal unless the dog is racing towards you. If you are sick of walking in different directions up and down the same piece of track, just remember it is all for a good cause. If you absolutely have to walk one way (to get back to the car, for example) then put the dog on the lead to do so.

Practise every day for at least a week, gradually reducing the frequency of rewards as follows:

- Day one: reward every recall

- Day two: reward nine out of ten

- Day three: reward eight out of ten

- Day four: reward seven out of ten

- Day five: reward six out of ten

- Day six: reward five out of ten

- Day seven: reward four out of ten

Stage five: obeying the recall command

It will only take a few days for your dog to begin to take it upon himself to check out your position more frequently each time you set off for a walk. No longer confident that you will follow him along without question, your dog will become increasingly convinced that you have become alarmingly unpredictable and need to be closely watched. Not only will he will be checking in on you far more frequently, he will also be staying closer to you during the walk. This is exactly the result that we want.

Now you have started to tip the balance of power back in your favour, you can start to find opportunities during the walk to work on your recall command. You are ready to recall your dog even when he is not already running towards you. Take care to call your dog only when the chances of success are high. Initially this means calling him:

- When he is close to you (five to ten yards)

- When there are no distractions (no other dogs or people visible)

- When he is trotting along at a normal pace (not going hell for leather towards the horizon)

- When his attention is relatively unfocused (not when he has his nose down an interesting rabbit hole)

This is more difficult than the previous stage, where we simply recalled the dog as he approached us. When we make an exercise more difficult, we increase the frequency of rewards, so you will need to make sure that you reward every one of these new recalls to being with. Diminish the frequency of rewards each day in exactly the same way as you did at stage four. When you have taken the rewards down to about a third of all recalls, you can attempt to recall the dog at greater distances. As always, increase factors of difficulty gradually and increase the frequency of rewards to begin with.

Maintenance

If you have worked through the above in the space of two to three weeks, you may be tempted to fall back into your old pattern of walking straight away. But to maintain the effects of the about turn walk technique you really do need to keep your dog guessing.

Try and fit in a lot of about turns in every walk for at least a month. Avoid dropping the about turns completely. You need to remain a little unpredictable. Your dog needs to know that while you may be a slow walker, you have a mind of your own and may not always be where he left you.

On some walks take jackpot treats and give them to him unexpectedly, when he obeys a recall. Sealed pouches of cat food are very handy to take on walks.

If your dog starts getting sloppy again, you know what to do. Just reintroduce the about turn walk and remind him that his job is to keep an eye on you, not the other way around.

CHAPTER 21

The Artful Dodger

It is very frustrating when your dog is just a few feet away but won't come close enough to let you put a lead on him, or when he dodges away when he sees the lead come out of your pocket. Many dog owners fall into the trap of teaching their dog that his lead is something to be avoided at all costs. They do this by unwittingly associating the lead with one of the most powerful recall punishments in existence: the end of the walk.

If you think about it from the dog's point of view, the end of each walk is a deeply unpleasant experience. Your dog has no concept of your priorities or the need to return home at some point in the near future. He doesn't actually need to go home at all. He only needs to be with you. To your dog, with his extraordinary sense of smell, his passion for exploration, his indifference to cold or damp and his complete lack of commitments, the great outdoors is a perfect paradise. It is a kaleidoscope of wonderful scents; a world of profound and delightful experiences waiting to be embraced.

To your dog, going home while there are still new scents to be explored, new trails to follow, new friends to meet and while he is still full of energy, is worse than pointless. It is a disaster. He probably feels as wretched at leaving the moors as you would feel if you had been transported to a tropical island paradise, given a suite in a five star hotel with your own private beach and then instructed to leave an hour later.

If the hapless dog owner creates an indelible link between this daily disaster and the simple act of putting a lead on his dog, you can see how the lead rapidly becomes a marker for the most unpleasant of punishments.

Prevention and cure

For those of you with a puppy still at the 'adoring his master' stage, you can nod and smile with just a hint of smugness. For you will never need to be in this situation. Preventing the birth of an artful dodger is as simple as one, two, three.

Each time you go for a walk with your puppy, recall him several times. More often than not, pop a lead over his head before you give him his reward, and then take it off again and let him run around some more. That's all it takes. If the lead is associated more often than not with some more freedom, an aversion to the lead will never develop.

But for those of you that already have a dodger on your hands, do not worry. This problem is fairly straightforward to treat. Within the space of a few short weeks, and often just days, you can teach your dog to love his lead again. If this is your only recall problem, you can simply use the following exercise on its own. But for best results follow it up by working through the Recall Training programme in Part Two. Please note that this short retraining programme is for dogs that come back when they are called, but do not like having their lead put on. It is not suitable for dogs that abscond (see chapter eleven) or when recall is faulty in some other way.

EXERCISE ONE **Feed on the lead (indoors)**

For several days put your dog on a lead to eat his dinner. You will have to stand there with him while he eats, but this is an important step. For best results, divide his daily ration into several portions at intervals throughout the day. Don't try and call or train your dog, or get involved in any conflict. Simply:

1. Go to the dog, pop the lead on (while he is indoors) as if you were going to take him for a walk

2. Feed, saying your new recall command several times while he is eating, and remove the lead when he has finished. You are building up a subconscious association between the lead and food / pleasure

Lots of small meals will hasten your success; doing this once a day will take you longer.

EXERCISE TWO Recall out of water

Still indoors, continue to feed the dog on the lead, but begin calling him to you first.

1. Recall the dog

2. Put the lead on the dog

3. Feed the dog

The more times you do this each day, the better. Give at least one jackpot reward each day (a sardine, a sausage or some warm cooked ham or chicken). Keep this up for several more days.

EXERCISE THREE I love my lead

Preparation for this step is crucial. The temptation for a dog to revert to his previous behaviour when released outdoors is very high. The longer you take on steps 1 and 2 the better your chances of success at this stage.

Preparation:

- Before the first outing, do not feed the dog for 24 hours. He needs to be hungry

- Take some exceptionally tasty jackpot treats with you (preferably cooked meat). Have plenty of it – you are going to be very generous

Method:

1. Take your dog into your usual dog walking area; a wide and open outdoor space where he is safe. Keep him on his lead

2. Wait until there are no other dogs, people or distractions nearby and feed the dog generously from your hand

3. Remove his lead

4. Let him run just a few steps and call him back with your new command. Put him on the lead and feed again.

5. Remove the lead and release the dog

6. Repeat steps 2 and 3 at least 10 times, letting the dog run around briefly in between, before taking him home. Don't let him go too far from you at this stage, and don't expose him to any distractions

What if it doesn't work?

If you have spent several days on each of steps 1 and 2 then you are unlikely to have problems at this stage. If you do, then an interim stage where you release the dog while he is wearing a training lead or check cord under his ordinary lead will help to condition the new behaviour outdoors. You will need to read chapter twenty-two, *Using a Training Lead*, before you use a training lead on your dog. All being well, you should repeat Step 3 daily for several days before proceeding to Step 4.

EXERCISE FOUR **Fading rewards**

It is important not to rush this step. People are often keen to remove themselves from their dependence on food rewards and fade them out too quickly. The old problem, if not properly extinguished, will resurface with a vengeance. The first step in fading the rewards is to replace some of your high-value rewards with more boring ones. Little cubes of cheese, toast or kibble make good basic food rewards with which to replace your tasty meat.

Reduce the high-value rewards gradually, over days or weeks. Your high-value rewards should continue to be used at least once during every walk for a couple of weeks, plus after putting the lead on to come home. Once you have the dog coming and willingly accepting his lead for simple rewards such as cheese or kibble, you can begin, just occasionally, to put on his lead without rewarding him at all. Continue to put the lead on and remove it many times during each walk.

Remember, you can never stop rewarding a dog altogether, if you do, the behaviour you desire will gradually deteriorate and you will be in trouble again. Don't be mean; when you take your dog out for a walk make the effort to take a treat or two along for him. It isn't much to ask.

CHAPTER 22

Using a Training Lead

The training lead or 'check cord' is a useful way of gaining some control over a dog while giving him the sensation of having some freedom. It can act as a kind of halfway house between wearing a short lead and running free.

There are a number of disadvantages to working with a dog on a training lead, but in many cases, especially with recall training, these are outweighed by the benefits.

Training lead facts

A training lead is a long line attached to the dog's collar or harness. It can be home-made but can also be purchased fairly inexpensively from online dog stores and some pet shops. If you buy one, choose a lead measuring at least thirty feet; shorter ones are not as useful. Manufactured training leads are generally made from a flat canvas webbing material which does not easily get tangled or snag on undergrowth, and is easier on your hands than a narrow rope. However, these webbing leads can be a little heavy for a small dog so you may need to improvise with some strong tangle resistant cord.

For very fast dogs, like greyhounds, you will need a longer lead. You may even need to tie two together.

Who needs a training lead?

If you are retraining a dog that has a history of absconding, a training lead is essential. Many dogs that become increasingly out of control need a training lead in certain situations. With any dog it is a good idea to have the dog drag a training lead if you are concerned about your ability to remain in control of the situation. As your confidence grows and your dog improves you can wean him off the lead at any stage in training. For many dogs this switch from dragging a lead to free running is best made at the very end of the training programme, when you have completed the proofing stages. You will know when you are nearly ready to wean the dog off the training lead because you will be going for days without needing to touch it.

For dogs that have had control issues, the training lead is an important tool. If you are retraining a dog that has previously had a serious recall problem, the training lead is indispensable.

What are the benefits of using a training lead?

In recall training, the long line or training lead can be used for three purposes:

- To prevent the dog from rewarding himself

- To get the dog's attention

- To prevent the dog from getting into danger

Preventing self-rewarding

In order to put an end to your dog's bad behaviour, he must not be able to engage in any activity that might be enjoyable to him immediately after committing an undesirable behaviour, such as ignoring your recall whistle.

You can use the lead to prevent the dog from helping himself to rewards such as chasing butterflies or playing with other dogs. Using a training lead in this way is essential for those that are retraining older dogs with a pre-existing bad habit; those starting from scratch with a puppy may be able to manage without one.

Getting the dog's attention

A little tug on the training lead may be sufficient to attract the dog's attention, in order to enable you to get him to chase you. More traditional trainers will go further and use a training lead to prevent the dog from avoiding a correction.

When you 'activate' a training lead by stepping on it or picking it up, you are preventing the dog from helping himself to a reward. A well timed 'no reward marker' can help the dog identify behaviour that is likely to result in him losing his reward. A sharp 'NO!' or 'AH AH!' is often sufficient to interrupt a sensitive dog that has not yet gained any bad habits. Remember to be ready to immediately engage the dog in some kind of activity after interrupting him in this way.

Keeping the dog away from danger

A dog wearing a training lead can be prevented from getting himself into dangerous situations, meaning you may be able to train in places that were previously off limits. A recreation ground with a road running along one edge, for example, might not be safe for your dog off the lead, but attaching a training lead to his collar might enable you to train and exercise him at a reasonable distance from any hazard.

What are the disadvantages of using a training lead? There are a number of potential problems. The main issues are:

- Safety

- Tangling

- Learned awareness

Safety

A key issue with training leads is safety. A lively dog may, at times, reach significant speeds. Anything that might bring the dog to an instant halt means that all his weight will be thrown at speed against whatever is restraining him. If this restraint happens to be a narrow collar around his neck, damage to the soft tissues of the throat can occur. For your part, trying to grasp a rope travelling at the same speed as the dog, in your bare hands, can result in very nasty friction burns. These problems can largely be avoided by correct use of the lead and by using the correct equipment for both dog and handler.

Ideally, a dog on a check cord or training lead should be wearing a harness. At the very least he must wear a wide flat leather buckle collar to distribute any impact over the largest area possible. Never attach a training lead to a slip lead or choke chain, or to anything else that might

Training leads should be attached to a wide buckled collar

be able to tighten around the dog's neck; nor on to a narrow collar that could cut into the dog's throat.

Don't be tempted to tie the lead to a solid object such as a tree or screw in dog tether. If the dog runs out of line at speed, the instant stop may flip him over and possibly injure him. Nor should the dog be allowed to swim on a training lead, especially where the water is deep or where there are currents. Our rivers and ponds are full of underwater hazards on which the lead may become tangled.

For your own safety do wear gloves when working with a dog on a training lead. Alternatively, you can make knots in the lead so that you can stop the dog by stepping on it. This will make the lead more likely to tangle though. Bear in mind also that it is not a good idea to attach the lead to yourself. A large dog can sweep you off your feet with shocking ease when he runs out of rope.

Tangling

Even with the best-made lead, snagging will occur in some situations. Using a lead in undergrowth or on very uneven or rocky terrain can cause snagging. Not only does this interfere with your training, it hastens the point at which the dog develops learned awareness of the lead, because he is constantly being reminded of its presence.

Good places to use a training lead are sandy or shingle beaches and the open grassland found in fields, parks and recreation grounds.

Learned awareness

It does not take forever for the dog to puzzle out that his potential for mischief off the lead is greater than his potential for mischief while he is wearing it. If great care is not taken, sooner or later many a dog will become aware that the lead is the source of your power over him.

It is therefore important that the trained response you are developing in the dog is deeply ingrained before attempting to replicate it with the dog running free. Should you attempt the transition too rapidly, the dog may make an error that he could not possibly have made on the lead.

If this happens on more than a couple of occasions, he will conclude that the lead is what is controlling him and from then on the dog will behave very differently running free than he will on the lead.

Avoiding awareness

To help prevent the dog from becoming wise to our cunning use of the training lead, there are a number of steps we can take.

We can have the dog:

- Wear the lead in advance of training

- Wear the lead throughout the training period

- Wear the lead after training is complete

We can also avoid touching the lead, stepping on it or letting it snag on anything at any other time than when we want to stop the dog; that is important in each of these three scenarios.

Wearing the lead in advance of training

A training lead feels very strange to the dog the first few times he wears it. He may try and shake it off or may pick it up and run around cheerfully carrying the end of it. But after a while the dog becomes accustomed to dragging the lead everywhere he goes and forgets all about it. It is at this point you can begin training on the lead.

Before this point, and before any training takes place on the lead, you must complete this period of acclimatisation, where the dog wears the lead a great deal and does not associate it with anything in particular. Use games or jog about, encouraging him to run along with you, to distract him from playing with the lead. If he likes to fetch a ball, keep him occupied with this for a while.

The important thing to remember is that the lead needs to become irrelevant to the dog. It needs to be something he wears often and that has no particular meaning. Initially, have the dog wear the lead in as many places as possible. You mustn't be tempted to leave the lead off because it is wet or muddy. Your lead will get very grubby, so don't even think about trying to keep it nice and clean. If you start to pick and choose where he wears the lead too often, the dog may figure out what you are up to.

Wear the lead throughout the training period

In addition to having your dog wear the lead in advance of the training period, it is helpful to have him wear it regularly throughout, and not just during the sessions or at the location you have set up to proof a particular skill.

Wear the lead after training is complete

Once the dog has grasped the skill you are teaching (recalling away from another dog, a jogger or children with ice-creams), you need to continue to leave the lead on for trips outside for some time. This ensures that the dog does not associate the lead purely with your training sessions, and that any slips or mistakes he makes in the first few weeks after you have finished proofing do not end in disaster.

Avoid pulling on the training lead

It can be very tempting to pick up the training lead and use it like a normal lead to get your dog to walk in a particular direction. Don't give in to that temptation. The objective is to avoid a situation where the dog runs out of rope and realises he is effectively constrained. With most dogs we achieve this by letting the lead trail along the ground for much of the time. With dogs that have a history of running away, spend a period of two or three weeks holding on to the lead during training sessions. This requires a little bit of practice because you will need to gather up the slack in the lead as the dog approaches you and let it out again as he moves away, while avoiding generating tension in the lead. It is quite a good idea to have a few dummy runs with a person holding one end of the lead and pretending to be the dog!

If your dog has no history of absconding, keep keep any handling of the training lead to a minimum. When you need to put your dog on a lead, to walk by a road or past a distraction you have not trained for, put a normal lead on him as well as his training lead. Mind you do not step on his training lead while he is walking next to you. When you are ready to let him go, just take off his normal lead and leave him trailing the training lead behind him. We want the lead to become background noise.

Activating the training lead

The only time you will be touching, pulling on or otherwise activating your training lead will be during a training session, to achieve a specific and pre-planned objective. Don't try to use the training lead to correct all manner of problems at once. Focus on your objective.

If you are using the lead to keep the dog in your zone of control, step on the end before he reaches the edge of your zone and try to attract his attention before he runs out of rope. If you can encourage him to chase you, or return without creating tension in the lead, so much the better. We do not want the dog to think he only has to return when the lead goes tight.

After activating the lead

If you have to use the lead to prevent the dog from taking off or doing his own thing, it is really important that you do not immediately put him back into a situation where he can fail again. After activating a training lead, always set up some easy exercises for the dog. Give him some simple 'sits' or 'downs', even better, take him into an enclosed area so that you don't have to touch the lead at all. Have several successful sessions on the lead before attempting the failed exercise again. The reason for this precaution is partly because it is demoralizing for him and partly because it will increase the chances of him working out the role that the lead plays in controlling him. If this is a dog that has been seriously playing you up in the past, he will be quite surprised that you were able to outwit him. Don't give him opportunity to figure out how you did it by running through the same routine again. Let him think you have grown some new and mystical power over him.

What if I failed to pick up the lead in time?

It happens. Sometimes we are taken by surprise and the dog shoots off before we have gathered our wits. I have done it and you probably will too.

So the dog is now heading for the horizon with his lead dragging along behind him. Please do not call him. If he were going to obey you, he would have done so before he took off after that rabbit. He certainly isn't going to now. Set off calmly after the dog and try not to cry. Jog if you have the energy, and focus on remaining very calm.

At some point you will get close enough for him to spot you. Now you must appear nonchalant. Avoid looking at the dog. Behave as though you have not spotted him. Scan the ground for the end of the training lead and walk calmly towards it. He doesn't know that this trailing device will control him and will probably think he is well out of your reach.

As soon as you are able to, step on the end of the lead and take hold of it. Encourage the dog towards you enthusiastically – do not get cross, despite having just run a mini marathon. Again, try to get him moving towards you before he runs out of rope. That way he will still not have been informed about the source of your power.

Remember, most importantly, your next job is to analyse what happened and make sure it does not happen again. Did you take the dog into a distracting environment without preparing him properly? Did you attempt to train too close to the distraction? Did you let your concentration drop? Did you let the dog get too far away from you (the most common reason for failure)? Work out where you went wrong and make a better plan for next time.

Dispensing with the training lead

In most circumstances the training lead is a temporary training aid. You use it to get through a difficult patch in training – usually where you are proofing against strong distractions or where you need to prevent the dog from approaching hazards.

It can be a great tool for dogs that have previously been serial absconders, but bear in mind that this sort of problem can take a very long time to solve. Your dog may need to wear this thing for up to a year. Don't attempt to rush it.

One way of fading out use of the lead without making an obvious switch from lead to no lead is to gradually shorten it. If you think you will need to use the lead again in the future and don't want to buy another, switch the lead you bought for some light old rope. As you almost certainly won't need to use it, it will just serve the purpose of the dog still feeling he is dragging something while you chop a bit off each day.

Remember to focus on the dog during your training sessions and to anticipate trouble. If the unexpected happens, don't hesitate to put the dog on a normal lead until the moment has passed. Train for one thing at a time and leave the training lead alone until you absolutely need to activate it. Then set the dog up to win next time.

CHAPTER 23

Getting Active with Your Dog

ike people, dogs get bored. The more interesting you are, the more you stimulate your dog's mind; the more you interact with him, the less boring he will find you and the mo re attention he will pay to you. So in this chapter we take a look at a range of activities you can participate in once your dog's basic obedience is thoroughly established.

Taking up a sport or hobby that you can do together will, in many cases, enable you to take his training to another level. This will further enhance your relationship with the dog, which in turn will be reflected by his attitude towards you when you are out and about. Some of the more physically demanding activities will help keep your pet in great shape, too. You can find more information about the activities outlined on the following pages at the back of this book.

Not all of the dog-related activities below are strenuous and if a more tranquil pastime appeals to you, you might be interested to know more about the Pets as Therapy (PAT) scheme.

The PAT dog scheme

The PAT scheme sends well-behaved, friendly dogs into hospitals and nursing homes to visit ill or elderly patients or residents; it arranges thousands of visits each year. The dogs and owners who carry out the visits are vetted to ensure that they are suitable visitors for vulnerable people, but the application process is fairly straightforward. Your dog doesn't need any fancy skills, just a relaxed and friendly temperament and some basic good manners. All PAT dog owners are volunteers and give up their time freely for this worthwhile cause. If your dog is fairly calm and very good-natured, you will be able to apply to act as a volunteer. The system is very flexible and PAT dog owners can pick and choose when and where they go and how many visits they make. You can find more information about PAT dogs on the PAT website.

The Kennel Club's Good Citizen scheme

The Kennel Club's (KC) Good Citizen scheme is intended to promote good basic dog care and training. It includes simple obedience and dog management skills and is divided into three levels of difficulty – bronze, silver and gold. The scheme is a good starting point for any new dog owner and there are training classes leading to good citizen awards in many towns and villages. With the techniques you have learned in this training programme you should find progression through the scheme quite straightforward, and your dog will benefit from opportunities to learn in a group situation. Alternatively, you might prefer to join a club that focuses on competitive obedience, which will enable you to take your training skills on to a much more advanced level.

Competitive obedience

Obedience competitions are run under the auspices of the KC. Any breed of dog can enter and though dogs do not have to be purebred or have pedigree papers, they do need to be registered on the KC's activity register. There are several levels of formal obedience test in the UK.

Dogs are tested on their obedience over a range of tasks and points are awarded by the judges for any performance that is less than perfect. The skills assessed include heelwork, recall and stay; the more advanced levels look at distance control and directions are included. The objective is to score a perfect zero, and the team with the lowest score wins.

Obedience training is a ring-based sport and while your dog won't be subjected to the distractions of the countryside, he will have to learn how to handle the distractions of a busy and possibly noisy arena.

To get involved in obedience competitions you will need to join a dog-training club that trains for these competitions. You can find more information about these on the KC's website.

Agility

Agility is a relatively modern sport developed around thirty years ago, but it has become a firm favourite both with participants and spectators. Dogs competing are expected to complete a kind of obstacle course, including a range of apparatus from see-saws to tunnels and jumps. Agility requires balance and coordination as well as good training and is popular with dogs of all sizes, though clearly the more agile the dog is, the better.

There is no breed or pedigree requirement for entry into an agility competition and dogs compete against other dogs of similar size. You would need to join a club in order to get access to the equipment you need for training for this fun activity. You can find out more about getting involved in agility online at www.agilitynet.com.

Flyball

Flyball is a fast, frantic and very noisy sport. The basic concept is that the dog runs down a narrow track and at the far end presses a spring-loaded plate that launches a ball. The dog then catches the ball and races back to the start line with the ball in its mouth. The game is run in relays and the fastest relay team is the winner.

Opposite page ▶ top: *Agility is great fun* below: *Collies often excel at Flyball*

Taking part in Flyball is very exciting and while all breeds of dog are eligible to enter, the competitions I have watched have been dominated by collie types, and there is a great deal of barking throughout. To find out more look on the British Flyball Association's website, and if a noisy arena is not your thing, how about the sport of CaniX?

CaniX

Going for a run with your dog isn't something you have to do on your own. An entire sport has developed around this activity, with organized runs or events being put on in different parts of the country. The sport is called CaniX or Canicross and it is becoming increasingly popular.

Any breed of dog can enter a CaniX event, although you have to be sensible about your dog's fitness and health. In CaniX dogs cannot run loose, even at heel, but must be attached to the runner in some way. Keen competitors wear special CaniX harnesses that allow their dogs to run in front while keeping their hands free. If you enjoy competitive running and are looking for activities to do with your dog, this could be just the thing for you.

Whether you run in events like these or on your own with your dog, remember to build up your dog's fitness gradually, just as you would your own – avoid running in hot weather when dogs can overheat. If your dog is getting on in years or has been unwell, have your vet check him out before beginning a programme of intensive exercise. A vet check is also important for brachycephalic (flat-faced) dogs such as bulldogs, as many may have breathing and cooling difficulties. You can find out more about organised CaniX events from the CaniXuk website.

Working trials

The sport of working trials is derived from military and police dog training techniques. Working trials is a challenging and strenuous outdoor activity that provides tremendous benefits in terms of physical and mental stimulation for dogs.

Dogs taking part are expected to master long jumps and high jumps, to retrieve anything (within reason) from a designated area and to track scent trails over long distances.

While any breed can take part, this is a sport for canine athletes and one at which Labradors particularly excel. You will need to join your local working trial club in order to participate and as the sport is overseen by the KC, you can get contact details from their website.

Gundog training

In chapter six, *Beyond Training*, I touched briefly on retrieving as an excellent activity to help you enhance and manage your dog's walks. If your dog enjoys retrieving and has some gundog genes you might like to consider going further and getting involved in gundog training.

Gundogs often make great family dogs. They are generally gentle, friendly and intelligent with a strong desire to cooperate with their human partners. Despite these features, gundogs also come equipped with some pretty impressive hunting instincts and these can be difficult to control if not managed effectively. Gundog training helps you to work in harmony with your gundog and to harness all that boundless energy and enthusiasm into a purposeful and controlled activity that provides both dog and owner with healthy exercise and a lot of fun. Importantly, the mental and physical stimulation also helps to keep your dog free of problem behaviours like running away, chasing wildlife and chewing up your furniture.

In the UK you don't need to actually go shooting in order to participate in gundog training. The Gundog Club runs a graded training scheme that enables pet and companion dogs to get involved too. The first four grades do not involve retrieving real animals or birds. Your dog does not need to be purebred to participate in the Gundog Club's graded training scheme, which is aimed at preparing dogs for gundog fieldwork and introducing pet dog owners to gundog training.

You can find out more about gundog training on the Gundog Club's website. You never know, you might enjoy it so much that you want to get involved with gundog fieldwork or even with competing in field trials.

Gundog training helps keep spaniels happy and out of mischief!

Field trials

Field trialling is the pinnacle of gundog work and one of the most demanding dog disciplines in existence. Field trials are competitions for trained gundogs and in the UK they take place under genuine shooting conditions. Each dog's ability to work, and to respond to his handler's command, is assessed by judges throughout the duration of a shoot.

Remaining calm and quiet under shoot conditions is very testing and all dogs competing must be capable of responding to whistles and signals at considerable distances. In the USA these distances have become extreme and American field trials are highly specialised long-distance retrieving competitions where dogs must be able to hold a line over extreme distances, which may include multiple water entries and re-entries. In the UK the emphasis is on finding game and steadiness under genuine shoot conditions.

If entering a field trial appeals to you, you will first need to train your gundog to a high standard, and to belong to a number of field trial clubs or societies. You will also need a dog that is registered on the Kennel Club's breed register and experienced in working in the shooting field. You can find more information about field trials, along with a list of clubs and societies, on the Kennel Club website.

Giving your dog a job to do

Dogs love to know what is expected of them.

One of the reasons that working dogs are so well behaved is that their options are always clearly defined. At any given time, the trained gundog, working guide dog or drug detections dog knows exactly what he is supposed to be doing; he is never milling around doing nothing and he knows how to behave politely around other dogs.

It is much harder for a dog to behave well if he has no real idea what is expected of him. Giving your dog a role to play, even if that role is simply finding a ball and bringing it back, is a valuable tool. Providing him with powerful rewards is another, which is one of the great advantages of getting involved with activities that your dog enjoys – it increases the range and value of rewards available for you to give him.

If none of these activities appeal to you, don't worry. You can maintain an excellent recall throughout your dog's life without rushing off to a club meeting or competition once a week; but unless your dog has a very placid and homely nature, you will need to take some steps to actively ensure he remains focused on you and under your control.

Try to follow the suggestions for the managed exercise in chapter six, and if you find your recall getting a bit sloppy at any time, spend a few weeks working on the about turn walk in chapter twenty. If you have had problems with your dog in the past, do read the first two chapters in Part Three, *Where Did I Go Wrong?* and *Out of Control?*, to give you some in-depth understanding of why some dogs are more difficult than others to control outdoors, and what can be done to help them.

We are almost at the end of our journey now. All that remains is the finish. Let's look at what happens when your dog completes his recall and see if we need to tidy things up a little.

CHAPTER 24

The Finish

We have come to the end in more ways than one. This chapter is also about the end or finish of each recall.

When an effective recall was just a distant dream, and your dog's disappearing rump a frequent reality, the manner of his return was irrelevant; you were just grateful to have him back at all. But now that your dog hurtles towards you at the first peep of your whistle, you may want to consider whether or not you are happy with the way in which he arrives at your side, or the way in which he greets you.

Barging past and jumping up

Many enthusiastic young dogs will approach their handler at an alarming pace, failing to brake effectively or to take avoiding action as they collide with your legs. I have seen people literally swept off their feet and onto their backs by young dogs barging into them in this fashion; it is a dangerous and disrespectful way for any dog to behave. You can prevent barging in certain situations by positioning yourself with your back to a wall or fence before recalling the dog, but this is very restrictive and impossible to do in some locations.

Some lively and enthusiastic dogs get into a habit of leaping and jumping all over their owners in excitement at the end of each recall. This too is not acceptable or appropriate behaviour, especially with a large dog.

As you move on with training, a temptation may creep in for your dog to become very perfunctory in his focus on you when he returns. This is especially true when we add some opportunities for fun into our rewards. For example, it is perfectly reasonable to reward a dog by allowing him to chase a ball, or to play with another dog after a recall. However, if we do this regularly the dog may rush his recall and barely give you a chance to touch him before he dashes off for another exciting game. While this dog is not such a hazard as the 'barger', a recall is obviously devalued somewhat if it does not enable us to touch or control the dog to any useful extent.

We certainly don't want to dent the young dog's enthusiasm for the recall, so we need to find a happy way to ensure he arrives in a more collected and dignified manner. Rather than trying to stop or correct the dog for behaviour that we don't like, it is usually more effective to teach him alternative and more appropriate behaviour. This means training the dog to carry out a specific action at the end of each recall that does not involve behaving badly.

Defining the finish

You have probably seen dogs in obedience competitions facing, and sitting neatly in front of, their handler with their nose pressed up against the handler's legs. This seems quite extreme to some of us, and very desirable to others. How you want your dog to present himself at the end of the recall is something of a personal choice. Bear in mind that sometimes you will need to give your dog some other instruction at the end of a recall, or to restrain him in some way. The minimum requirement for any recall must be that the dog remains near to his owner for long enough to allow the owner to give another command, or restrain the dog using a lead if necessary.

Here we look at two different types of finish to a recall that you might like to consider – the hand touch and the front sit.

The hand touch

One way to complete a recall is to ask the dog to press his nose into the palm of your hand for two or three seconds. This method has the added advantage of presenting a clear visual signal to the dog. This visual hand signal can also become an effective recall command in its own right.

The hand touch signal is the open palm of the hand (fingers together) facing forwards. The trainer's arm hangs down at their side, and is straight and fully extended.

The touch itself is simple and quick to teach. You just need to give the dog a reward marker for each successful nose touch, and then gradually increasing the duration of the touch that the dog must sustain before marking and rewarding his actions. A verbal reward marker such as 'Good!' or 'Yes!' will suffice.

A three-second nose touch gives you sufficient time to take hold of the dog's collar with your other hand if you need to restrain him or attach a lead.

Start by teaching your dog to touch your hand repeatedly at home without distractions and then add the recall on to the hand touch in stages as explained on the following pages.

Presenting your hand

In the following exercises, you will present your hand target to the dog for a limited time, and then return your target hand to a neutral position (e.g. elbow bent and forearm resting across the front of your body), with the palm away from the dog. Choose which hand will be your target hand and stick to it. Before you start a training session, give your marker word 'Good!' followed by a treat; do this two or three times in succession to get the dog interested in the game and paying attention to you.

EXERCISE ONE Assisted hand touch

In the first exercise, you will make it easy for the dog by moving your hand nearer to his nose if necessary. Have some treats ready, and your hands in 'neutral'.

1. Present your target hand and count to five

2. Mark ('Good!') and reward any touch of your hand by the dog's nose.

3. If the dog does not touch within five seconds move your target hand close to the dog's nose for a further five seconds

4. Mark and reward any touch of your hand

5. Put your hand back into neutral as soon as the dog has touched your hand or when your five seconds is up

Present your hand in this way at least ten times, marking and rewarding any successful interaction with your hand. If you are struggling to get that first touch, rub a little cheese on your target hand to make it smell 'good' and try again. If the dog is using his open mouth rather than his nose, you will need an interim stage where you hold your palm angled above the dog's nose to ensure a nose touch rather than a mouth touch.

Soon the dog will be moving to touch your hand with his nose during the first five seconds and not waiting for you to move your hand towards him. When this happens, move on to the next exercise.

EXERCISE TWO Solo hand touch

This is just the same as exercise one but this time you won't help the dog by moving your hand near his nose. You will present the hand target by your side and he will need to get himself close enough to you to make the touch.

1. Stand close to the dog. Have your treats ready and your hands in neutral. Be ready with your marker word or clicker

2. Present your hand and count to five. Keep your arm extended and your hand by your side

3. Mark and reward touch of your hand by the dog's nose

4. Put your hand back into neutral

If he does not attempt to touch your hand, make no comment, just put your hand into neutral and try again. Repeat until the dog can do five successful hand touches in a row. If he struggles go back to exercise one for a while and then set up a halfway house exercise where you push your hand forwards a little bit to encourage the touch.

Now practise in different rooms in the house. Do several sessions of ten to twenty touches. When your dog is confidently and rapidly offering a nose touch every time you present your target hand, you can build a little duration and persistence into this new behaviour.

EXERCISE THREE Double hand touch

In this exercise we will not reward the dog or return the hand to neutral after the nose touch; we will leave the hand there for a further five seconds.

1. Present your hand and count to five

2. When the dog touches your hand, start counting to five again

3. Mark and reward the second nose touch

4. Put your hand back into neutral

Most dogs will offer a second touch if you don't reward the first one. If the dog seems confused, push your hand a little nearer to his nose but discontinue that as soon as possible. Repeat until your dog is offering lots of double touches. Keep watching the dog closely because sooner or later he will offer a longer nose touch or the two touches will become merged into one. Mark and reward. This is what you are waiting for.

Gradually become more demanding. Drop the rewards for briefer touches, reward for longer ones. Aim for two seconds first, then three. If you don't seem to be getting many longer touches go back to the double touch for a while. You do not need to be too fussy. The objective is simply for the dog to touch your hand in a deliberate way, and for long enough that you are able to take hold of his collar if necessary, or to give him further instructions.

The front sit

If you would prefer to teach your dog to sit in front of you at the end of each recall, then you will need to teach him a nice reliable well-proofed sit of at least five seconds in length. Proof the sit thoroughly in different situations and with different distractions, just as you did the recall, then begin to add the recall back on to it as explained below.

Adding the recall to your finish

When you begin adding a recall to your finish you will need to start with tiny short recalls.

If you teach your 'barger' a simple hand touch and then launch straight into a fifty yard recall, he is not going to remember the hand touch, no matter how obvious your hand signal is. He will be travelling at twenty miles an hour and his head will be full of nonsense. All thought of touching your hand will desert him as he approaches you and you will have set him up to fail.

So, begin with very short recalls. Try three yards. Call the dog and as he approaches make your hand signal as dramatic and obvious as possible. Do NOT reward the dog if he fails to touch your hand immediately. Remove your hand and turn away from the dog; then turn back to face him and give him the hand signal again. Reward generously when he gets it right; repeat over shorter distances if he gets it wrong.

The same applies if you are asking for a sit but because there is no visual signal you will need to give a verbal one. Call the dog from just a few feet away and tell him to sit before he actually touches you. Reward profusely if he sits without bumping you, turn your back on him if he barges you and try again with even shorter recalls until he gets it right.

After a few successful repetitions, try dropping the sit command. Just wait and look at the dog without speaking or offering a reward. Most dogs will offer you a sit at this point, which you can mark and reward generously. If not, just practise for a while longer. You can try dropping the sit command another day. Once the dog is offering you a nice sit at the end of each short recall, with no prompting, you can start to build up distances.

Increase distances gradually, a few feet at a time, and shorten up in new locations. Take your time. Avoid too many errors. If the dog is denied rewards too often as he recalls over and over again his recall will suffer. So make sure that the recalls are short enough for him to succeed with the hand touch or sit most of the time. With some dogs you may need to begin at just a couple of paces away. Just as with the recall, do all these early practices in the house, and once you have begun to attach your tidy finish to short recalls, build up distances gradually at home and in the garden; then start all over again with short distances outdoors in different locations.

Work in stages, as always, rewarding generously in each new location and fading rewards to an occasional treat over time. Whichever finish you choose, remember to insist on it for every recall from now on. Be absolutely consistent and your dog will not let you down.

Of course, if your dog is not a barger or a dasher you may decide to dispense with the finish entirely. On the other hand, you may decide to go even further and play around with something fancy like a sit in front, followed by moving around behind you and finishing in the heel position. While in no way essential, these types of trained skills are more than just a bit of fun. They build up your dog's attention span, keep him from getting bored and help to focus your dog on you as the person who guides him.

If you find you enjoy this kind of training and want to do more, there are lots of resources on the Internet to support you and many good training clubs that will help you and your dog delve deeper into the joys of obedience training.

Pass it forward

I can't believe that we have come to the end of this book. It's been quite a journey, and I would like to thank you for sticking with it to the end. I do hope that you have had some fun along the way.

Sadly, dog ownership is a responsibility that many people secretly find a considerable burden on top of all the other demands of modern life. Many dog owners don't know how to get results with kindly training methods. They want to avoid old-fashioned and punitive techniques, but don't have sufficient understanding of how rewards work to use them effectively. As a result they accept life with a large animal rampaging irreverently around their home and the countryside as a natural consequence of bringing a dog into their lives. It needn't be this way.

Living with a dog should be a pleasure, and understanding how dogs learn through consequences, and how we can control those consequences, is the key to enjoying our dogs. None of the information in this book is new or groundbreaking, much of the research from which it is drawn has been available for many years, yet despite the resources now at our disposal, dogs are still widely misunderstood.

One of my aims in writing this book was to show that modern training methods needn't be confusing or complicated, and that it is worthwhile getting inside your dog's head and working out what makes him tick. The benefits of reward-based training go far beyond a simple trained response, and I hope you are now feeling the advantages of an improved relationship with your dog.

Do recommend this book to anyone that needs it, and let's make sure that more people get to enjoy the thrill of seeing their dog galloping home towards them as fast as their legs will carry them.

Useful Resources

If you are keen to find out more about dog training, or how dogs learn, here are some useful resources.

Books

Books about how dogs think and learn

The Culture Clash by Jean Donaldson
James & Kenneth Publishers, 1996

Don't Shoot the Dog by Karen Pryor
Bantam Books, 1984

Books about problem dogs and problem behaviours

When Pigs Fly by Jane Killion
A book about training 'difficult' dogs
Dogwise Publishing, 2007

Oh Behave by Jean Donaldson
A book about problem behaviours in dogs
Dogwise Publishing, 2008

Basic dog training

How to Teach a New Dog Old Tricks by Ian Dunbar
Basic dog training and management skills, with health and diet
information included
James & Kenneth Publishers, 1996

Clicker Training for Obedience by Morgan Spector
A very detailed book about shaping basic behaviours for competitive
obedience
Karen Pryor Clickertraining 2004

Gundog training

The Right Start by Pippa Mattinson
Passing Grade One by Pippa Mattinson
Passing Grade Two by Pippa Mattinson
Passing Grade Three by Pippa Mattinson

Guides to raising a gundog puppy and early training for pet and working
gundogs. Available directly from the Gundog Club

Photographs

Many of the images in this book, including the cover photo, were provided
by professional dog photographer Nick Ridley
www.nickridley.com

Additional photographs by professional photographer Jeff Boston
www.jeffbostonphotography.co.uk

Online Resources

Acme Whistles: www.acmewhistles.co.uk
The world's largest and most famous producer of whistles

Websites for dog activities

The Kennel Club: www.thekennelclub.org
Good Citizen scheme, obedience competitions, working trials,
and field trials

The Gundog Club: www.thegundogclub.co.uk
Gundog training for pet and working gundogs. Gundog field tests.

Agilitynet: http://www.agilitynet.co.uk
The birthplace of agility

British Flyball Association: http://www.flyball.org.uk
Information about competing and training for Flyball

CaniXuk: http://cani-cross.co.uk
International CaniX news and events

Pets As Therapy: www.petsastherapy.org
Charity that arranges visits made by PAT dog volunteers

Websites and blogs about dogs and dog training

The first two sites are my own.

Totally Gundogs: http://www.totallygundogs.com
A website dedicated to gundogs and gundog fieldwork

The Labrador Site: http://www.thelabradorsite.com
A website and forum dedicated to Labrador health, training and welfare

The Dog Star Daily: http://www.dogstardaily.com/blogs
A busy dog news and information site featuring articles by a range of
respected behaviourists and dog trainers

Karen Pryor Clicker Training: http://www.clickertraining.com/
Information and helpful articles on clicker training and learning theory

Index

Index subheadings in *italic* are named exercises

About Turn Walk 44, 65, 75, 203–8
absconders 67, 191–200
    bonding through training 193, 194–5, 196, 200
    corrections, avoiding 200
    food rewards 195–6, 198–9
    hand feeding 196
    new habits, building 199
    retraining the recall 197
    safety issues 193, 200
    training leads, using 67, 193, 197, 215
activities with your dog 58, 62, 224–32
    see also games
age-related disobedience 173–4
agility training and competitions 62, 226
association, learning through 42, 43, 75, 83–4, 85, 87–8, 95–6, 102

bad behaviour, rewarding 176–7
Basic Recall 92, 104–16
    distractions 105, 109
    failure analysis 109–10
    indoor recall 105–14
    new room recall 108–9
    one man garden recall 114–15

outdoor recall 114–15
    recall from food 111–12
    recall from room to room 109
    recall from sleep 110
    recall speed 113–14
    rewards
        premium rewards and jackpots 106, 113
        random 107–8, 113
        same room recall 106–7
behaviour modification 16, 21, 23, 24, 39
behavioural science 16, 18–29
biddable dogs 33, 89
bonding with your dog
    puppies 65, 92
    rescue dogs 57, 195
    through training 169–70, 193, 194–5, 196, 200
    weakening the bond 202

CaniX (Canicross) 228
challenge method of learning 50
chase recall 188–9
chasing
    handler chases dog 31, 176–7
    instinctive 24, 56, 61, 66, 181, 183–4, 185–7
    puppies 43, 83–4, 87, 89, 176
    self-rewarding through 56, 62, 66, 181, 184

supervision and control 62, 167, 186–8
switching chasing instinct onto handler 31, 32, 62, 74, 87, 148, 167
check cords *see* training leads
conditioning 75, 88, 95, 102, 166–7
    operant conditioning 26, 28, 35, 36–7, 38, 151
    see also association, learning through consequences
    delayed 23
    punishers 27, 30, 32
    reinforcers 27, 28, 184
    taking control of 24–5, 26, 28, 40, 57
    timing 22–3, 39, 178
    see also punishment; rewards
control issues 66–7, 180–90
    see also absconders; chasing
corrections 31–2, 216
    absconders 200
    side effects 31–2, 40

delayed consequences 23
disobedience *see* naughtiness, concept of
distractions 51, 90, 142–4, 156–63
    diluted 160–1
    fake scenarios 50, 77, 160, 161
    levels of 52, 157–9
    practice exercises 162–3
    unexpected 163
dog trainers 19, 20, 23, 31, 37, 50, 77, 130
    see also gundogs, training
dominance 23
drives 24
    see also chasing

exercise requirements, daily 193
extinction (behaviour) 26, 168
    controlling 26, 27, 44
extreme conditions, recall under 78, 168

family and friends
    interference with training process 45, 105
    working with 76–7, 87, 117, 124, 130, 133, 161

finish of a recall 233–9
    adding the recall to a finish 238–9
    assisted hand touch 235–6
    barging 233–4, 238
    defining the finish 234–5
    double hand touch 237
    front sit 238
    hand touch signal 235–7
    solo hand touch 236–7
flyball 226–8
food rewards 32, 33–4, 195–6
    accessibility 34–5
    basic 71
    bonus 72–3
    bribes 37–8, 102
    changing to non-food rewards 167–8
    choice of 34
    food-indifferent dogs 34
    jackpots 38, 73
    lures 102
    mega 73, 198–9
    premium 72, 106
force fetching 28

games 59–61, 66–7, 168, 185, 187, 196
generalised learning 15–16, 44, 49, 168
    see also proofing the recall
gundogs 24, 56, 59, 139, 183–4, 186, 189
    field trials 231
    training 28, 62, 185, 187, 229–30

habits, building good 67, 78, 137
hand feeding 196
houseline 130–1
hunting instinct 24, 56, 61, 66, 181, 183–4, 185–7
    see also chasing

instinctive behaviours *see* chasing; hunting instinct
intelligence, canine 20–1
interacting with your dog 58, 59–61, 62, 63, 65, 187, 188
    see also activities with your dog; games; managed exercise

Kennel Club's Good Citizen scheme 225

leadership 23–4
leads
    artful dodgers and 209–13
    as recall punishment 209–10
    fading rewards 212–13
    feed on the lead 210–11
    I love my lead 211–12
    see also training leads
luring your dog towards you 42–3, 74,
    89–90, 119, 145, 147–8
    food lures 102

managed exercise 59–62, 66–7, 75–6,
    187, 188, 231–2
motivation
    self-motivation 77–8
    your dog's 16, 20, 24, 77

naughtiness, concept of 21–2, 48, 49,
    53, 174
    age-related disobedience 173–4
negative reinforcement 28
novel situations 168

obedience training and competitions
    225–6, 234
older dogs 94–103
    bad habits, countering 95
    moving dinners 100
    moving treats 100–2
    new recall command 95
    pre-recall training 95–6
    retraining 65–6, 75–6
    whistle equals wow! 96–7
    whistle means dinner or wow 98–9
operant conditioning 26, 28
    gambling effect 35, 36–7, 38, 151

pack theory 23–4
past history of your dog 56–7
Pets as Therapy (PAT) scheme 225
physical punishment 8, 14, 30
problems, anticipating 62, 163, 164
proofing the recall 41, 43–4, 48–54,
    116–55
    advanced strategy 156–65
    basic concept 129

distractions *see* distractions
effectiveness 53
failure to proof the recall 48–9, 180
group training classes 164
necessity for 49–50
on location 141–55
    choice of location 142, 143, 151
    come away from a loose dog 146–7
    distractions 142–3
    engaging with your dog 144–5, 154
    fading rewards 151
    lead walking 147, 154
    long running recall 149
    longer standing recall 150
    recall failure 147–8
    recall out of water 152–4
    rewards 144
    short standing recall 149–50
    slow responses 148
    two man recall 151
    'warming up' exercises 145–6
proofing with dogs 128–40
    assistants 129–30, 133, 139
    come away from a dog on a lead 131–2
    come away from a loose dog 136
    come away from a moving dog 134–6
    dog trainers, help from 130
proofing with people 116–27
    assistants 117
    come away from a boring person 117–18
    come away from a different assistant
    122–3
    come away from a friendly person 120–1
    come away from a person with food
    121–2
    come away from a visitor in the garden
    123–4
    two man garden recall 125–6
    rewards
        fading 119, 139
        random 124
    what it is 49
punishment 30–2, 33, 39
    corrections 31–2, 40, 200, 216
    impracticalities 31, 40, 50, 77
    physical 8, 14, 30
    poor timing 178

punishing the recall 76, 124, 179–80, 192, 209–10
side effects 31–2, 40
verbal 27, 31, 32
puppies
bonding with 65, 92
chase response 43, 83–4, 87, 90
learning to love the lead 210
safety response 82–3, 86, 90
puppy recall 82–93, 173
association, learning through 83–4, 87–8
failures 89–90
follow my leader 85–6
involving family members 87
older puppies 94–5
recall and run 89, 90–1
recall and walk 90–1
rewards 85, 86–7, 88
tripping hazard 87
unfamiliar places 90
whistles are great 84–5

recall failure 172–80
dealing with 70, 109–10, 119, 147–8
puppies 89–90
training errors 175–80
young dogs 173–4
recall signal 41–2, 44–5
new signals 44–5, 65–6, 75, 95–6
pairing with recall behaviour 42–3, 75, 83, 84, 85, 87–8, 88, 92, 144
selective use of 54, 62, 66, 75
single use of 70, 92, 126
verbal 45, 47
see also whistles
recall speed 113–14, 148
Recall Training Programme 41–7, 69–70
associating the recall signal 41, 42
establishing recall behaviour 41, 42–3
maintaining the recall 41, 44
obeying the recall signal 41–2, 106
objectives, defining 160
staying committed and focused 77–8, 164, 188
structured training 15–16, 82–170

training reviews 167–8
training strategies 70–1
see also older dogs; proofing the recall; puppy recall
reinforcers 27, 28
continuous schedule of 36
diminishing frequency of 29, 35
negative reinforcement 28
variable schedule of 36, 37
see also rewards
rescue dogs 17, 57, 181, 191–2, 195
see also absconders
retrieving games 59, 66–7, 168, 185, 187, 196
reward markers 74
'no reward' markers 216
verbal 32, 85, 107, 235
reward-based training 15, 28, 30, 34, 39, 41, 77
rewards
effective 32–3
fading 88, 89, 90, 212–13
failure to reward 175–6, 213
food *see* food rewards
high-value rewards 66, 71
non-food rewards 38, 66, 73–4, 178, 179
poor choice of 178–9
poor timing 178
random 29, 36, 37, 88–9, 113, 124
rewarding bad behaviour 176–7
stroking/patting 32–3, 89, 178
see also self-rewarding

safety issues 61, 193, 200, 216, 217–18
scents, distracting 51, 56, 143
self-rewarding 26, 52, 56, 58, 62, 66, 70, 177–8, 181, 184
preventing 177–8, 215–16
through chasing 56, 62, 66, 181, 184
sloppy recalls 44, 65, 75, 167, 191, 201
see also recall failure
sociable dogs
distractions 51
proofing the recall
with dogs 128–30
with people 116–27

sociable dogs *contd.*
  restricting interactions with other
    dogs 137–9
spaniels 33, 56, 181–3, 184–5, 187
supervising your dog 57–8, 61–3
  managed exercise 59–62, 66–7, 75–6,
    187, 188, 231–2
  trouble, spotting 62–3
  zone of control 61–2, 145, 200

temperament of the dog 55–6, 65, 173–4
training classes 164, 187
  see also gundogs, training
training diary 145
training leads 61, 62, 67, 130–1, 164,
    177–8, 188, 189, 190, 193, 197, 214–23
  acclimatisation 219–20
  activating 216, 221–2
  choice of 214–15
  fading out use of 164, 222–3
  handling 220–1
  houseline 130–1
  learned awareness of 218–19
  losing hold of 222
  occasional use of 220
  purposes 215–16
  safety issues 216, 217–18
  snagging 218
  trailing 220
  weaning off 215
training programme *see* Recall Training
    Programme

training reviews 167–8
verbal rebukes 27, 31, 32
verbal recall signals 45, 47
verbal reward markers 32, 85, 107,
    235
visitors to your home 122–3, 124

walking to heel 61–2
walks
  about turn technique 44, 65, 75,
    203–8
  dog 'check-ins' 202, 203
  dogs running ahead 202–3
  interacting with your dog 58, 59–61,
    62, 63, 65
  managed exercise 59–62, 66–7, 75–6,
    187, 232
  supervising your dog 57–8, 61–3, 167
water, recalling from 152–4
whistles 41–2, 45, 46
  command recognition 41–2, 43, 45
  pairing with recall behaviour 42–3, 75,
    76, 83, 84, 88, 92, 144
  pips 46–7
  stags horn whistle 46
working dogs 139, 228–9
  see also gundogs
working trials 228–9

zone of control 61–2, 145, 200